YOUTHFORCHRISTUMZANSI

ANOTHER CHANCE

How often we wish for another chance to make a fresh start.

A change of failure into winning.

It doesn't take a new day to make a brand new start

It only takes a deep desire to try with all our hearts

To live a little better and forgiving and to add a little sunshine to the world in which we are living in

So never give up in despair and think that you are through, for there's always a tomorrow and the hope of starting new

Hush, little sister
Please don't cry
I wish I could be there
To sing you a lullaby

I can see your arms
Bloodied and bruised
That's strange, little sister
Mine were like that too

I know you scream
When Daddy's there
Hush, little sister
I know you're scared

I can see the way
He's hurting you
I'm sorry, little sister
He did that to me too

I know that people
Ignore what's going on at home
That makes me angry, little sister
You shouldn't have to be alone

Hey, little sister
You want to know why I'm not there?
It's a sad story, little sister
But people should care

You see, little sister
One day Daddy got high
You were asleep in your crib

So you didn't hear my cry

He screamed at me
And smashed my head against the door
While you slept, little sister
I died on the floor

You know, little sister
I don't think that I would have died
If someone had only bothered
To listen to my cries

But hush, little sister
Daddy's coming home
Quick, get into bed
You don't want him to find you alone

I'm sorry little sister
He's in a bad mood
Run while you can

Uh oh little sister
He's lifting his belt
Scream while you can, little sister
Call for help

Hush little sister
You don't need to cry
No one can hurt you
You're in my arms tonight

.

Mlungisi MAKHANYA

DIGITS
ONE OUT OF EVERY **THREE** GIRLS

WILL BE SEXUALLY ASSAULTED

BY THE AGE OF **EIGHTEEN**

ONE OUT OF **SEVEN** CHILDERN

IS ABUSED

EVERY **ONE** MINUTE

HOW MANY DO YOU KNOW?

FIVE TEN FIFTEEN?

CAN YOU AFFORD TO IGNORE THIS?

TWENTY-FOUR HOURS IN **ONE** DAY

I PRAY FOR YOUR FORGIVENESS

SEVEN DAYS IN **ONE** WEEK

I PRAY FOR YOUR REPENTENCE

FOUR WEEKS IN **ONE** MONTH

I WANT YOU TO LOOK INTO THE MIRROR

TWELF MONTHS IN **ONE** YEAR

I HOPE YOU REALISE WHO YOU SEE

THREE HUNDRED AND **SIXTY FIVE** DAYS

I HOPE AND PRAY FOR YOUR TRANSFORMATION

IF YOU ARE **ONE** HEARTLESS PERSON

I PRAY FOR YOU TO SEE

AND BE AFFECTED BY THIS **ONE** MESSAGE

FOR ALL OF US

IF YOU ARE AFFECTED BY THIS

IF THIS MESSAGE IMPACTS ON YOU

AFTER READING IT

I ASK YOU TO PASS IT ON

AND MAKE OTHERS READ IT

MAKE **FIVE** COPIES OF THIS AND PASS IT ON TO OTHERS

NKELELE COMMUNICATIONS

My heart bleeds

My heart bleeds and there is no containing my blood

I am tormented by the same love that I believe in

Stressfully I await your insult

I have met all your relatives

Insomnia, poor libido, headache, backache, ulcers

Where do you want me to stop?

I see you and I am not angry

I am saddened by your behaviour

You are a small child in my eyes

You are seeking attention

It got you lashing out at me

I do a self introspection and there you are

You are big part of me

Why? Do I love you?

You remind me of sorrowful life

You are so vindictive

You are revengeful

You are full of hatred

You excite over my sadness

Why are you with me?

Do I love you? Why?

It is like the lamp is shattered

There is no more light

Darkness just engulfed my non-jungus senses

The river just went dry on me

My chest aches for pure water

My cells feel like bursting on me

I now understand the concept of the outcast

You made me one cutting from life

You gave me you but you are an opposite of me in all ways

Will you ever change?

Do you it? Is this why you hate me?

Make me understand because I see love in you!!

You are not the monster you make yourself to be!!

Am I wasting my time believing you will change?

You make my heart bleed eternally!!!!!!!!!!!!!!

REAP WHAT YOU SOW
SOW **ABANDONMENT**

REAP **SUFFERING**

SOW **ACCOUNTABILITY**

REAP **MATURITY**

SOW **ACKNOWLEDGEMENT**

REAP **RECOGNITION**

SOW **HONESTY**

REAP **TRUST**

SOW **LOVE**

REAP **HAPPINESS**

SOW **ANTAGONISM**

REAP V**IOLENCE**

SOW **AVARICE**

REAP **DEATH**

SOW **WOMANISM**

REAP **DECEIT**

SOW **DISGRACEFULNESS**

REAP **BLACKSHEEPNESS**

SOW **EFFICIENCY**

REAP **BOON**

SOW **CAGINESS**

REAP **LONESOMENESS**

SOW **FRIENDLINESS**

REAP C**ANDOURSOMENESS**

SOW **GOODNESS**

REAP **HARMONY**

SOW **BADNESS**

REAP **GRUDGES**

SOW **OBSCENENESS**

REAP **SHAME**

SOW **HUMOUR**

REAP **KINDNESS**

SOW I**NFERNO**

REAP **GRUESOMENESS**

SOW **SELFISHNESS**

REAP **REPULSIVENESS**

SHORTY

SURE I LIVE IN THE FLAT

BELIEVE ME I GOT THE GAME

BUT I`M NO FLIRT

YOU ARE JUST MY DAME

I AM NOT THE WORST

YOU ARE NOT CHARMAINE

YET I AM NOT LIKE WEST

YOU DON`T DRINK CHAMPAGNE

YOU SWEETER THAN STAMBO

I SAW YOU IN SPAIN

WHENEVER YOU SAY JUMBO

YES THERE COMES RAIN

ALL IN ONE WEEK

YOU ARE NO ALICIA KEYS

LEAVING ME ALL WEAK

YET, YOU ARE MY KEYS

YOU ARE ABSOLUTELY ROUND

NO BEGINNING OR ENDING

I FEEL LONELY IF YOU NOT AROUND

LIFE GOES ON

TUPAC WAS RIGHT

LIFE GOES ON

THEY ARE NO MORE

SO, FILL THAT POSITION AT WORK

ACCEPT THE NEW PERSON

NO ONE ASKS YOU TO FORGET

NOT EVEN TO CRUMBLE

BUT TO REMEMBER NOW AND THEN

REMEMBER TO SURVIVE

YOU ARE NOT ALONE

THOUGH HE IS GONE

SO SAID MICHAEL JACKSON

FAMILY CAN`T BE REPLACED

GIVING SOMEONE SPACE

DOES NOT MEAN BEING FORGETFUL

REMEMBER THE GOOD TIMES

DON`T FORGET TO SMILE

SHE MAY BE GONE

GIVEN UP ALL HER DREAMS

JUST BECAUSE OF YOUR LOVE

YOU FEEL EMPTY AND LONESOME

GO ON AND MOAN

LOVE DOES NOT DIE

LOVE GOES ON

THE RING IS NOT FULL

THE CHAIN OF FRIENDS LOST ONE BEAD

THEY ALL MAKE A BID

I AM NOT A FOOL

THEY CAN`T REPLACE OUR FRIEND

FILLING HIS SPACE

WON`T MAKE US FORGET

WE ARE ALLOWED TO REMEMBER

YET LIFE GOES ON

SHE HAD AN IMPORTANT ROLE

OUR TEAM HAS NOW GOT A HOLE

THE BALL PASSES ON

THEN IT FALLS DOWN

SHE`S NO MORE TO CATCH IT

WE NEED SOMEONE IN THE GAP

FOR LIFE GOES ON

HE`S NO LONGER ON THE BOX

WE NO LONGER LAUGH

PLANTS ARE DRY

HE`S NO LONGER THERE TO WATER THEM

CHILDREN ARE MISERABLE

THEY ARE WITHOUT TOYS

LIFE GOES ON MY PEOPLE

SOMEONE MUST TAKE OVER

MYLOVE

Darling, you are **Angel**

I came to Cape **Town**

Because of you my **Angel**

I cannot be of the T**own**

Not without you my **love**

I do not want to be **part**

Of something hurting our **love**

Which is why, I'm off the **part**

You see I love **you**

Straight from my **heart**

I will always love **you**

You will always be in my **heart**

LIFE and LOVE

LIFE IS ABOUT DARE

HOW WE GO ABOUT LIVING ABOVE CHALLENGES

LIFE IS ABOUT PEOPLE WHO LOVE US

HOW THEY HELP US THROUGH OUR CHALLENGES

LIFE IS ABOUT US ALL REACHING OUT TO GOD IN ONE DARE

LIFE IS ABOUT MAKING USE IN FULL COMMAND OF RESOURCES GIVEN TO US

LIFE IS ABOUT MIXING RESOURCES TO MAKE THE BEST OF LIFE AS WE KNOW IT

LIFE IS NOT ABOUT WORLDLY MATERIALS

THEY CAUSE STRESS IN A PERSON

HATRED CAUSES MUSCLE TENSION MAKING THE SKIN UNNATURAL

LOVE RELAXES YOUR SOUL MAKING YOUR BODY LOVABLE

THE MIND IS THE SOURCE OF CONNECTION, IT NEEDS TO BE FREE AND POSITIVE

AVOID THE BAD PAST, IT CAN EASILY DESTROY THE GOOD THING

DEEP IS NOT SHALLOW, DEEP STAYS FOREVER, SHALLOW WASHES AWAY EASILY

I LOVED YOU BECAUSE WE CONNECTED MENTALLY AND SPIRITUALLY

I LOVE YOU BECAUSE WE ARE HAPPY TOGETHER, YOU MY SOURCE OF LAUGHTER

I WILL ALWAYS LOVE YOU BECAUSE YOU MY BEST FRIEND

LIFE WITHOUT YOU IS A MESS WITH NO TENDERNESS

I LOVE YOU BEING YOU JUST YOU ONLY YOU

YOU ARE ME AND I AM YOU

TOGETHER WE ARE UNTOUCHABLE

TRUST IN ME AS I TRUST IN YOU

I`M JUST SAYING, SERIOUSLY

YOUR EYES MESMERISE THIS MAN

HE WANTS THE TWO OF YOU TIGHT

HE CAN`T HELP BEING UPTIGHT

YOU ARE UNDER THE SKIN OF THE MAN

YOU POSSESS A BEAUTIFUL SMILE

IT MAKES HIS SORROW GO AWAY

YOUR LIPS HAVE THIS BEAUTIFUL LINE

THIS MAN CAN`T HELP BUT KISS YOU

YOUR BREAST INVITE THIS MAN TO BE CLOSE TO YOU

HE IS PANTING HEAVILY, THAT`S NO LIE

GOD KNOWS YOU ARE LOVED

LOVED MORE THAN YOU`LL EVER KNOW

GOT TO GO HERE COMES THE SNOW

HOW CAN I GO WHEN THERE`S THIS FIGURE

SLIM FIGURE GOOD HEART IT POSSESSES

YOUR HIPS MAKE ME HOP

I BREAK MY NECK, AM IN POSSESSION

AM I IN THE POSITION

IS THERE ANY HOP`

WHAT IF I TOLD YOU, LET YOU KNOW

WOULD YOU HOLD ME IN YOUR ARMS

WOULD YOU HAVE TOLD ME

LET ME KNOW THAT YOU LOVE ME

WOULD YOU LET ME IN YOUR ARMS

`CAUSE HERE I AM IN THE COLD

NOTHING CAN MAKE ME HOT, NOT EVEN WARMTH

THOUGHTS OF YOU MAKE ME WARM

I KEEP HEARING YOUR NAME

MY MIND CAN`T STOP THE CALL

I LISTEN TO YOUR MUSIC COLLECTION

FOR A MOMENT YOU'RE HERE

YES OF COURSE I CAN HEAR

YOU LOUD AND CLEAR

YOU ARE LIKE A BLUE SKY

YET YOU ARE NOT SO SHY

IN YOU I FIND PEACE; YOU ARE MY PIECE

YOU FULL OF TRUST; I AM IN LOVE

YES YOU ARE MY SOUL MATE

I AM YOUR FOREVER MATE

TRIBUTE TO KHANYISA COMMUNITY CHURCH

HAPPY ARE THOSE WHO BELIEVE WITHOUT QUESTION

UNHAPPINESS SHALL THEY NOT KNOW

READY FOR ETERNITY ARE THEY

CHRIST IS THEIR LORD AND SAVIOUR

HOLLY GOD KEEP SAVE THEM

CALLING ALL GOD`S CHILDREN

IF WE ARE GOING TO SEE THE MASSES

SWEPT INTO THE CHURCH

WE MUST REMEMBER THE POOR

AND WHAT`S MORE

WE MUST BE EAGER TO DO IT

BECAUSE THERE ARE NO WELL-TORN PATHS AHEAD

TOGETHER YOU`LL MAKE A ROAD

THAT OTHERS WILL FOLLOW

TOGETHER YOU`LL ACCOMPLISH

WHAT YOU COULD NEVER ACCOMPLISH ALONE

KHANYISA I HAVE GROWN TO UNDERSTAND YOU

HAIL TO THE GOD YOU PRAISE

AMEN TO THE PRAYERS MEANT FOR THE POOR

NOT ONE SOUL GOES HUNGRY FROM YOUR CHURCH

YES YOU FEED US THE WORD OF GOD

I AM FREE IN YOUR PRESENSE

SELFLESSLY I GIVE MYSELF TO YOUR PROGRAMS

ALLELUJA TO JESUS IN HEAVEN

CANDLE THAT BURNS IN OUR HEARTS

OF COURSE YOU GIVE US LIFE

MANY KNOW GOD THROUGH YOU

MANY ARE IN HEAVEN BECAUSE OF YOU

UNITED WE STAND AGAINST SATAN

NOTHING CAN TOUCH US

IN GOD THERE IS TRUTH

TILL THE END OF THIS WORLD

YES WE GIVE GLORY TO GOD

Tribute to Nelson Mandela

Noble and Honourable
Every Nation salutes yeah

15

Long live Madiba
Socialist Nationalist Africanist
Oh my leader
...Never dying in spirit
RMC existed for you
Hell broke loose coz of you
Oh! no you people were never on sale
Long live Rholihlahla
Indeed you`re a role model
Heavens will open up for you
Long live Nelson Mandela long live
Amandla! Awe Africa
Madiba unqobe iRobben Island
Awaze wadayisa ngathi kumabhunu
Deliberately tempting you
Invading your inner soul
breaking you into pieces
Amazingly you resisted
Making sure we are free
Amandla!Awethu

Nelson you my leader
Democracy we finally enjoyed
eventually we are free
Long live the spirit of Freedom
Aluta! Continua!

H2O

Rolling thunder

Randomly **stormering**

Destroying life

Eyes full of fire

Anguish and rage

Never been seen

Death only Bodily death

From the mountains

They came down **streaming**

Shining from afar

Beautiful by sun`s rays

No, no menace

Only life

Bodily life

From the fields

They were **riverring**

Dark and quite

Pregnant with anger

Deep in anguish

Only death

Bodily death

By hand of man

They went **damming**

Tail between the legs

Hiding fury and rage

Tamed like a domestic hound

Only life

Bodily life

Naturally from underground

They came **larvaring**

Boiling ready for roast coffee

Idling thundering roaring

Letting it all out

No, no more life

Natural couriers

They are **searing**

Bringing it all

To the sea

No life

Only death

Total bodily death

TIME TO CHANGE

HEY YOU, YAH YOU

WHY ARE YOU SO SAD

DON`T YOU KNOW

YOUR TIME HAS COME

YOU ARE SUPPOSED TO BE HAPPY

GOD HAS SPOKEN

AND WANTS YOU TO CHANGE

STOP WORRYING ABOUT THINGS

THINGS THAT YOU HAVE NO CONTROL OVER

ONLY HIM CAN DO SOMETHING

ABOUT THEM AND CONTROL THEM

YOU HAVE DONE YOUR PART

BELIEVE ME IT HAD AN IMPACT

`TIS TIME TO LET HIM DO HIS PART

HE CAN DO MORE IN YOUR LIFE

JUST LET HIM FILL YOUR HEART

LET HIM TAKE CONTROL OF YOUR LIFE

WITHOUT HIM YOUR LIFE IS NOT WHOLE

YES HE IS ALFA AND OMEGA

SELFISHNESS

The ability to trust, love, help,

Care, support, and be happy with,

Think4, indulge in, laugh with,

Experience, give power to,

Trust, be sweet to,

Partner with YOURSELF.

Being able to do these

And much more for yourself

Teaches you to do them

For and to OTHERS

BE SELFISH 4 GOOD!!

JESSICA DAYRODRIGUEZ

JEALOUS ALONE YOU ARE MY INSPIRATION

EVERY WORD IS PURE AS GOLD

SAY IT AGAIN

SAY NOT FOR GAIN

INDEED YOU ARE SPECIAL

ASK ME I`LL TELL THE TRUTH

DO NOT ASK ME

AND YOU WILL NEVER KNOW

YES YOU INSPIRE ME

REALLY YOU OPENED MY EYES

OH JESSICA GOD KNOWS

DO NOT HESITATE

REACH OUT AND TOUCH

INDEED YOU`LL BE SAVED

GOD LIVES IN ALL OF US

UNLESS WE BELIEVE

EVIL WILL BENEFIT FROM US

ZEAL AND ZEST WILL LEAD US THROUGH

QUOTATIONS

"WINNERS NEVER QUIT, QUITORS NEVER WIN"

"FRANKNESS AND SINCERITY ALWAYS FRIGHTEN PEOPLE A LITTLE,THEY GET A FEELING THAT YOU MIGHT GO TOO FAR"

"WITH A DIAMOND AT HAND SHE JUST DISSOLVED ON HER SEAT SHE SUCCUMBED TO HIS ILLUSSION AND GAVE UP EVERYTHING"

"NEVER ASK A DOG TO GUARD A BONE"

"Sometimes the only person you can trust is yourself"

"Life is not about waiting for the storm to pass, it is about dancing in the rain"

"Behind every bitch is a guy who made them be"

"Think I`m tripping tie my shoes"

"Never make someone your everything, when they are gone you got nothing"

"Smile because it is the second best thing it can do"

"You may not be perfect but you are you"

"Never regret something that once made you smile"

"You can give me kisses and hugs, I only want love"

"Words left unspoken are ones that often break hearts"

"There may be 1000 000 reason to give up, but you are one reason why I keep trying"

"I love you is easy to say and difficult to do"

"The painful thing is to see someone you love; love someone else"

"Never mind people ill speaking of you behind your back, you`re a couple of steps ahead"

"Anyone can make you smile, anyone can make you cry but a special person will make you smile with tears in your eyes"

"God damn I am good in bed I can sleep for days"

"I smile because I have no idea what`s going on"

"If you were to ask how many times you ran in my mind, I would say once because you never left"

"Better be hated for who you are than to be loved for being someone you are not":

"Love never walks away but people do"

"Loving someone who doesn`t love you is like loving a cactus the tighter you hold the more pain you feel"

"Never cry for the same reason twice"

"While you follow your heart, take your brain with you"

IT`S ALWAYS BEEN YOU

YOU'LL ALWAYS OWN MY HEART
WE HAD SHORT TIME IN DA SUBSTATION
NEVER THOUGHT YOULL BE THE FIRST TO GO THOUGH
WELL, WHAT CAN I SAY GOODBYE MY LOVE
...IT'S TIME I SWITCHED OFF THE LIFE LINE

NO, IT WAS NEVER YOUR FAULT
THE MAN ABOVE IS IN CONTROLS
HE KNOWS WHAT GOES IN
HE KNOWS WHAT COMES OUT
YOU DID COME IN
ASTONISHINGLY YOU WENT OUT FIRST
ILL BOW OUT MYSELF SOMEDAY
MAYBE THEN WE WILL BE ETERNALLY TOGETHER

THE HEART OF A WOMAN

TIS THE MOST CUNNING AND CARING
HEAVEN IT SEEKS IN DARKNESS
EVIL SHE TRIES TO AVOID IN VAIN
...HANDS TOGETHER IN PRAYER
ETERNITY IS THE HOPE
AVOIDING THE SIN IS ULTIMATE
REVIVAL IS FOUND IN THE BIBLE
TRUST IS UPON THE MAN OF GOD
WILL POWER IS THE HURDLE
ONLY HER LOVE IS THE ENEMY
MAN OF HER DREAMS
AH YES HES NO GOOD
NOT AS GOOD AS THE PRIEST

THE LAMP IS SHUTTERED

INCREDIBILITY RAN THROUGH MY NON-JUNGUS SENSES
HEARING DAT THE ALTER WAS DARK
THE WORD WAS NO MORE, JC FLEW
...THE LAMP TO GIVE US LIGHT IS NO MORE

THE RIVER OF LIFE JUST WENT DRY
THEREZ NO MORE H2O
SOUL CELLS R CRACKING
DESERT JUST VISITED US
IS THIS THE VICIOUSNESS YOU PROMISED US
CAN'T U REMIND US WHAT WE FORGOTTEN
DO WE HAVE TO BE IN THE HOLE FOREVER?

TRIBUTE TO MAFIAHILL MESSIAHS

ALREADY I KNOW YOU ARE THE BEST

THE WORLD WILL KNOW YOU LIKE WEST

RIDE ON MAKE WAY FOR THE BRIGHTEST

INTERNATIONALLY YOU ARE WISEST

BEST HIP HOP SONG IN ITS LONGEST

UNDOUBTEDLY SMOOTH AND DOPEST

THE GAME AGREES DREAMS SO BIGGEST

EVEN WWW WORLD HEARD `BOUT YOUR GREATEST

TRANSITION TO THE WORLD WIDE WEB OF COOLEST

OMARIOS TUPACS LIL WAYNES KANYES AND THE BEST

MUSIC INDUSTRIES HAVE EVER SEEN

AH! AH! NO YOU HAD NO SIN

FEEL ME! `TWAS NEVER FORESEEN

IN FACT BETTER ASK RITSON

AND SNOOP CAN CONCUR IN BRICKSON

HEAVENLY GETTO IS FOR THE NEVER BEEN SEEN

INDEED THEY HAVE NO SIN

LIL WAY KNOWS HE LOST TO EMINEM

LET HIM SAY "I AM WHAT I AM"

MAY BE WE ALL MAY BE SEEN

EVEN IN THEE BRIGHTEST

SELLING SPOTS OF THE GREATEST

SINGERS AND RAPPERS

I BELIEVE WE WILL HEAR YOUR COOLEST

AND LONGEST I MEAN THE LONGEST

HIP HOP SONG IN THE WORLD OF THE BEST

SINGERS AND RAPPERS--------------GREATEST

I`LL BE THERE

We don`t realize what we have till it`s too late

By then it`s gone and done for!

I know I did my share of mistakes

I learnt from them though

Can`t you see? I`m doing this for you!

Will be there when you need me

I am your shoulder to cry on

I wanna be the one holding you in my arms

I wanna be the daughter you dreamt about

Sorry if I live up to your hopes

I am me not someone else

I can`t change who I am

Can`t go back to living in the past

Too painful, I know you had it not easy too

Both of us need to realize

What`s gone is gone, we can`t go back

Let`s look forward

Never let this chance pass us

I`ll be there when you need me

I`ll be there when you cry

You don`t have to ask

No matter what happened

I`ll be there by your side

Only if you let me

MY DADDY IS IN HEAVEN

People ask me why I kneel down in your name

I tell them I miss you

They say my dad is alive at home

I say my daddy has always been in heaven

I was with Him and I will be with Him

That place is beautiful and peaceful

My daddy is more like me

I sometimes sit and cry looking in the mirror

I have changed from what He is

I wipe the slate clean

Start afresh to be like Him

It is difficult in this world

My daddy has always been in heaven

He has no wife, used Mary to carry me His only son

I will one day be beside Him

One day I will suffer no more

Hatred will never touch me

Death will be conquered

BACK IN MY LIFE

So many nights, I ask myself the same question

Did not know we would grow so far apart

So close yet so distant

So unsure if we`ll ever find each other again

I can`t go on

I need you back in my life

I tried so hard for you to see

You don`t even recognize me

How can I go on pretending?

Everything is alright; knowing you gone!

I want you back in my life still

Can`t imagine where this leads to

Don`t want you to realize too late

That I`m trying to get you to where we were

`Tis difficult because you not bringing your part

This is tormenting my heart

I want you; need you right next to me

As I'm standing here I keep thinking

I see our dreams that we had

They are shattered now, all gone with the wind

Why am I still hanging on?

Desperate and falling

Can`t you see?

Come back; let`s try again

We can`t` give up now, you know

I need you back in my life

I WANNA LOVE YOU

Can I kiss on your cheeks?

Move slowly towards you smooth lips,

Caress them with my tongue,

Move down your neck towards your tight breasts,

Wow, hear you moan,

You breathe heavily on my chest,

I am on your belly button with my tongue

You want to tell me something

But words are lost in the sensual feeling,

I carry on to your soft hairless unders

So tender and warm,

I caress it with my tongue,

Inside it goes, you moan deeply,

"Please go in further" you say.

I can taste your orgasm with my tongue,

Taste good, finally I put myself in,

You so warm and tender,

Slowly I move along with you,

Slow strokes that are inviting

And finally after a long twenty minutes I cum,

"I came 8 times" you tell me

ALWAYS MY BRIGHT ANGEL

Snow just filled the room

Everything smoggy white

Still you are so clear

Bright as the eastern sunshine

Loveliest of my heart

Pirates is the sign

Love is the action

Face so shiny

Blushing with love

See that sign behind you?

Yes it is all love

Sunshine bright with rays

One love brings us close

Together we strong

The cross reminds me of the pain

Mel, why did you remind me?

It was all fading away

Yes you raise it up

Made me go through it again

But you my angel shines

Heavens open up

Just at your gaze

You my shining angel

I CAN`T FACE YOU NOW

I am so ashamed of who I became

Like a brainless persona am longed hair

Shrinking skin I`ve developed

MY clothes torned into pieces

Beside the shops I beg for a cent

Just to get myself a fix for a day

Inside the rubbish bin my food is packed

Like an obidoxime I am the victim of the weather

Spotty is better than me

His owner had him a shelter built

Rains and hot sunny weathers

All befriend me; not knowing how I really feel

All night I cry wish for the morning to buy me a coat

Sunshine comes and I tell myself

"What a waste of last money buying a coat

When it is hot" at night I cry once again

I steal risking me to be beaten to death

If not having my ass jugged

Just to get my daily coke

How I tremble without it?

My eyes are so bolshie, can`t see straight

Can`t even face you

I hate what I deformed to be

I don`t know how to pull myself off the muddle

I am sinking deep into trance

There is no coming back

COLD HEART

How beautiful you look

Yet how alligatored are you?

You full of ice even your shadow is arctic

You so frigid you don`t feel

I want you to be close to me

What do I get a very insensate shoulder?

I sometime think you are a Anglophobe

But you my sister, how can you execrate me

Are you melting?

No I don`t think so

Cold hearts never melt

They only get snowier

ANGEL OF THE NIGHT

HOW I AM AFRAID OF THE DARK

UNDER MY PILLOWS LIE FROGS

I SCREAM IN MY DREAM

"NIGHTMARE" A SOFT WORD WOULD TELL ME

I LOOK UP AND SEE YOU ANGEL

MY ANGEL OF THE NIGHT

NIGHT CRAWLERS SICKEN ME

SEA SICK ON LAND I BECOME

YOUR GAZE RESTORES MY STRENGTH

YOU MAKE IT ALRIGHT

"JUST PUSSY CAT CRAWLING IN THE ALLEY"

YOU WOULD TELL ME

THE WHEEZING WIND

MOVING DOORS AND SQUEECKING WINDOW

THE GHOST HAVE COME TO VISIT

"IT WILL TAKE ME LIKE IT DID MY FATHER"

WITH A TREMBLING VOICE, I TRY TO TELL YOU

YOUR WARM HANDS HOLD ME CLOSE

SECURED I FEEL IN YOUR ARMS

BLOOD SWIMMING POOL

RUSSIA HAS IT GOOD

THEY ARE RED IN OCTOBER

UNLIKE ME IN SOUTH AFRICA

IM SWIMMING IN THE RED POOL

THIS IS A POOL OF BLOOD

IM SWIMMING IN THE POOL OF BLOOD

MATHEW GONIWE CONTRIBUTED TO THIS POOL

HECTOR PETERSON CONTRIBUTED TO THIS POOL

76 SOWETO STUDENTS CONTRIBUTED TO THIS POOL

LOTS OF MY PEOPLE MADE A CONTRIBUTION TO THIS POOL

WHERE DID CHRIS GO TO?

WHO SAID "MAMA TELL MY PEOPLE THAT

MY BLOOD SHALL NOURISH THE TREE

THAT WILL BEAR THE FRUITS OF FREEDOM"

THIS IS THE BLOOD SWIMMING POOL IN WHICH

THE BLOOD OF MR AND MRS MXENGE LIVES

IT IS THE SAME POOL IN WHICH MANY OD MK CADRES`S BLOOD LIVES

SOLOMON MAHLANGU, QUOTED YOU ABOVE

YOU SACRIFICED YOUR BLOOD FOR THIS SWIMMING POOL

MY FREEDOM AND YOURS WAS OBTAINED THROUGH THIS BLOOD SWIMMING POOL

YOU THINK FREEDOM IS GOLDEN

YOU THINK FREEDOM IS IN THE HOLE

YOU THINK FREEDOM IS PERSONAL WEALTH

NO, FREEDOM IS SACRIFICE

FREEDOM IS LETTING GO OF YOUR MOST PRECIOUS STONE

FREEDOM IS TO SPILL BLOOD

FOR THE SAKE OF OTHER PEOPLE

SENSELESS SHOUTING NEVER EARNED ANYONE FREEDOM

ANGER NEVER EARNS ANYONE FREEDOM

BUT BLOOD SWIMMING POOL

PEOPLE`S BLOOD

WE ARE SWIMMING IN THE BLOOD SWIMMING POOL

WE ARE FREE!!!!!!!!!!!!!!!!!!!!!!!!!

WHY?????????

WHY A WOMAN MUST CRY OVER A MAN?

WHAT IS IT THAT MAKES A WOMAN SHED TEARS?

WHY MUST A WOMAN CLOSE HER EYES AND CRY?

SO MUCH TORMENT

THE SPARKLES WITH GLITTER

YET THE WOMAN CRIES OVER A MAN

SOMEONE WHO THINKS OF ANOTHER

OPEN YOUR EYES AND SEE

SEE THE BEAUTY IN FRONT OF YOU

FEEL YOUR HAIR MOVING

THE SEA BREEZE REFRESHES IT

YOU CAN`T FEEL IT

YOUR MIND IS GONE THE OTHER SIDE OF TOWN

THROUGH THE SKY`S GLAZE

I CAN SEE YOUR BLUE TEAR FALLING

YOU GAVE HIM ALL

NOW THAT HE IS GONE

YOU HAVE NOTHING

YOU ARE EVEN WITHOUT YOUR SMILE

WHY WOULD YOU DO THAT?

RIGHT HERE IN FRONT OF YOU

AM ALWAYS IN YOUR GAZE

YOU CAN`T SEE ME

THOUGH, WHY?

AFRICA

Africa oh my Africa

Why do you like Xenophobia?

What good do you derive from abhorrence?

When will you learn to be allegiant?

We are of the same Motherland my Africa!

Mountains and hills

Bushes and trees

The whispering grass

Waterfalls, rivers and springs

They all make the beauteous Africa

Frolicsome you are my Africa

Fifa is conscious of you

Eufa boasts your advances

IRB adores you

The International cricket community feels you

Netball, Hockey and lots more you possess

Swimmers and Athletes come from Africa

Why worry about those who look down on upon you

Dark they say you are

Bright all over you are

I love you my Africa

Africa my beginning Africa my ending

O GOOD AND UNENDING

Lindsay Athiemulam
Tidal wave of departure smashing on memories
With a plunk it erases the forever that she dreamed of
Drenched is her red dress
Drops falling are fading dreams
Tidal wave of departure smashing a friendship
Washing away her love, like a last wave good bye from a window on a train.

No return ticket, tidal wave of departure washed it away

Molly Maharaj
We Are One
In this play called Life
Our parts unfold, each a roll to complete
The end is fixed, the rest may re-set
For the Playwright gives u the freedom to decide
So with each dawn, another chance is born
With each day a chance to recover
Make your moments be moments to treasure
When this play is over
God Bless us all, One Nation, One People, In God

Rassool Snyman
Who Will Cry When Humanity Has Gone?
Who will cry when humanity has gone?
Who will lament
Who will grieve?
Who will call her name?
In sorrow
As the dirge passes
The gods shall bow their heads and weep
At the demise of the man creature
For he had within him seeds of greatness
But he chose self destruction
The universe shall hold its breath
The nightingale will be silent
The butterfly shall shed her wings
The stars will be pensive
The moon will cover her face in grief
For those on whom she cast her silvery glance
Have gone forever
Who shall cry when humanity has gone?
The earth will ask
There will be but silence
For there are none left to weep?

Pius Mpk
My Definition

We can define politics in many ways as Human beings

If we would be able to hear what other beings would define it
We may not agree with or visor versa
It's like a jungle war fare where u have to use all u can to survive
Even if it takes you to be more wild than the others
Or be perceived stupid and looked down upon
But if you're the weakest link the strong will shine over your dark night
Like the moon and stars prevailing above you!

Lindsay Athiemulam
Tidal wave of departure smashing on memories
With a plunk it erases the forever that she dreamed of
Drenched is her red dress
Drops falling are fading dreams
Tidal wave of departure smashing a friendship
Washing away her love, like a last wave good bye from a window on a train
No return ticket, tidal wave of departure washed it away

Jude Joneson

Come away with me
Let me soothe your troubles let me ease your pain
Let me taste your innocence
Let me smell your soul
Least I take you through fields unknown
Come away with me
Let me transport your mind to another height
Let me take you there let it last all night
Feeling your senses
Touching your mind
Easing your tensions
Moving in rhyme...
Come away with me
Let me make you mine

Rassool Snyman

Of Hidden Treasures

I saw her in the fields of whitened bones
Moving from dead corpses
To living ones
Peering deep into closed minds and open breasts
Seeking her lost treasures
Calling their names woefully
The mists softened her face
And hid her tears
Her shadow wept silently into her hands
As her dreams grieved
In spaces where all emotions had died

Her eyes darted here and there
Searching sorrowfully
For the elusive thing she treasured and called truth
How far she had travelled
From time immemorial
To isles beyond time
Cosmic clocks stopped ticking
As she passed
As their hearts broke at her grief and loss
The universe cried starlit tears
That fell to the earth in glittering showers
That streaked the skies
With shimmering lights
How the gods must have stared
As pain was wrapped in exquisite beauty
The fairies marvelled
Swept in waves of ecstasy
The dervishes whirled
In deeper understanding
Of the universe and its deeper truths
Rumi stood entranced
As Gibran wrote
Upon the skies
His truths as he saw them
But she saw none
As truth
Her long lost treasure
Was lost somewhere in the ether
Of material lies
And biological illusions
That confused the reality
With reality
The earth songs was sung
As the angels danced
In celestial mansions
Where eternal truths resided
Incense wafted through the air
And soft chanting filled the air
Comets fell like scattered prayer beads
Rolling through minds and souls
Of the man creature
Who never knew truths?
Even as they stared at him in his dreams
And waking moments
God bless the child

Who knows the truths?
And sings his song to the universe
In the voice of eternity
One day
When time sets
On the horizon
His mother shall stop her lament
And beam with joy
Such is the tale of hidden truth
And the mother wanders the fields
Of whitened bones
And dead dreams
Such is the tale of searching mothers
And hidden truths

Rassool Snyman
Uhuru: A State of Being

The killing fields of Marikana lie naked
Bare
Cold
Only ghosts of the tragedy
Wander hither
Thither
To and fro
Wringing their hands
And moaning softly
Political opportunists position themselves
New jackals replacing old jackals
But the killings will continue
If not today
Tomorrow
The slave master is a wily beast
Who chooses his servants well
A sly puppet master who plays his puppets to deceive the people
And lead them to slavery once more
Political figures
Like well trained marionettes
Sing and dance before the people
Lulling them to sleep
And hypnotising them with fancy rhetoric
Whilst wealth and freedom is yet denied
Or delayed
The bankers wear their blood drenched suits
And friendly empty
For none see their role
Of creating money from the dreams of the people
And pressing them further into poverty
And despair

The IMF
The World Bank
And the Reserve Banksters
Are the old oppressors wearing new faces?
With new partners
Who dance upon our dreams?
Wearing diamonds on the soles of their feet
And watches that cost more than our homes
Or dreams
Woe to the people of Africa
Children of despair
Of deceit
And exploitation
Until the minds eye opens
And deceitful leaders are seen for what they are
Living in Sandton
Whilst the people live in Alexandria
The puppets will change
But the exploitation will continue
Heed well the words of Lumumba
Sankara
Subukwe
And Nkrumah
For in their wisdom the pointed to the path
That we must take
Lest the jackals change
And the people remain in chains
Uhuru now
Is the mantra for us and our children?
The slave master must leave
And take his puppets with him
Uhuru is not just a word
An act
It is but a state of being
That Africa must begin to live
The jackals position themselves
The people must be wise
Uhuru is not just a word
An act
It is but a state of being
Serpent Seven

Usually I can hide my feelings
Tucked away under this frame
Far, far away from all to see
This time it's different
Proud but, full of pain
Confused, stained
Wishing, praying it doesn't end this way

And yet I smile, because God, I'm so happy for you

You're doing so well, despite my complexion so pale
I wouldn't have it any other way!

So, I use my usual defence, and bow away
Silent, and in pain
I won't show a tear, call, or point blame

You are forever woven into my heart
Imbedded, connected
Even long after it stops, you'll still own it

Piece, by piece... Part by part

Dear Chris Hani, the communists are all dead

DEAR Mr Chris Hani

I write to you in response to the letter

Mr Zwelinzima Vavi of Cosatu wrote to you on the 19th anniversary of your assassination

That we have given to writing to the dead must give you a good sense of how bad things are in this country

The thing is, Mr Vavi's letter is too economic with the truth

As a good black person, I cannot let the dead be misled

Firstly, Mr Vavi approves of Nelson Mandela's call for peace and turning your death into a pressure point for a day of election

Sir, I would have thought that as a good student of Vladimir Lenin, Vavi should know that revolutionary communists have little respect for bourgeoisie liberal democracy

Therefore, Madiba should have turned the civil war into a revolutionary war to seize power and usher a new order, instead of betraying what good communism stands for through his call for elections instead of revolution

Mr Vavi mystifies the policy choices the ANC alliance has undertaken in the past two decades and the devastating impact they have on the poor

As soon as the ANC took power, it abandoned the already watered-down Reconstruction and Development Programme (RDP) and fully embraced the National Party's economic policy under the name "Gear".

Vavi and Cosatu made half-hearted protests, and then during the next elections called upon the victims of Gear to vote ANC

This has been the trend ever since. Vavi doesn't tell you the e-toll he bemoans and calls upon workers to protest against is a policy of his comrades in the ANC.

Rumour has it that even Cosatu is a beneficiary in the privatised roads system.

Yes, workers are militant; but Vavi makes sure the militancy is used towards reformism and is calculated to support the factional fights within the alliance for the control of the state to eat by the tender.

Mr Hani, the drill to power to realise one's own personal security through self-enrichment is what drives the battles in the ANC

The reason why we are having this problem of communism that is dying in SA is because our Comrades in the ANC and SACP believe more in tenders than state having its own capacity to deliver services, they outsource service delivery.

Comrade it is so bad that Comrades drive around the country with bags full of money from tenders. Comrades Chris I hope you were here to see that are Ministers are not fired because they can't deliver, the get fired because they are involved in tenders.

Comrades, the houses that our comrades build for the poor, I am sorry to make a comparing, but apartheid builds bigger and better houses for our people. The Education system is producing matriculants that can neither write nor read.

Comrade Chris, do you know that our roads have been privatised? Comrade Chris our townships have been turned into retail outlets. They have built big malls in our townships and the spaza shops are suffocating

Mhlengi KaMtungwa KaNdaba

Jude Joneson
Looks like I'm getting a second chance to love and be loved
Life works in mysterious ways
when I first met him he was in a relationship with another
I had no inclination of anything but I just thought he was sexy
time past and we joked around and had some fun and began talking
as simple as that we found we have many things in common
life isn't always about trying to be the prettiest or the sexiest because in fact most men just want a real woman
Someone to be their companion to share their life with from day to day
someone who does not give them drama
God sent you to me and I know that we were made for each other
My only advice for those who always miss out on love is quit trying so hard
It is somewhat a whirlwind courtship our wedding date is set for my birthday
We are going to live the rest of our lives together and grow old together and have so much fun doing so
I love you my sexy Richard with all my heart

Chele Hummingbird

Sometimes my man`s a dreamer
with plans to reach the stars
But he spends more time hustling' tit
in sleazy smoke-filled bars
An' you can find him anytime
when he's not here with me
Pourin' whiskey in his beer
feelin' wild and bein' free
But after all the moneys spent
an' he feels all alone
he bids the barroom girls goodnight
an' blindly staggers home
He knows that I'll be waitin'
He figures that's my place
He don't know how much it hurts
To miss his ugly face

An' he don't know how proud I feel
to party by his side
An' when he leaves me here alone
he don't know how I cry
But don't think I don't love him
just cause I get upset
You gotta know I love him
~ I HAVEN'T KILLED HIM YET! ~

Jessica DayRodriguez

A fire circle of flame adores her
with the brightness that reveals all the concealed
Creating dew drop kisses as she leaves by his warm light
for in this life, the Moon reserved all her passion and her sweetness for him alone
while leaving a cold chill that fills each night

... As I am the Guardian Sky of this sacred distant love
high within the starlight they share above
The Sun rests comfortable in my lap, as waking one side of the world
and I hold up the Moon to shadow the other side for a night nap
Only I can touch the intense purity of love being who I am
yet my sky eyes weep filling the ocean and streams of the land
Knowing that I am in between this constant battle of dark and light
my thunder roars and my lighting strikes devouring an emptiness I know within me
Only to return to happiness leaving rainbows for each
A bittersweet twist still. as each reaches for the other with no end in sight.
One with the morning and the other with the night
For when they wish to touch
they will only feel in their hearts they cannot enter within
nor will they be able to leave either without
Her shadows comfort his world as he brings forth her light
I don't pay attention to the smoke clouds they create
knowing they are just the steam from their flame
Winds gust as they blow each other kisses around
knowing each Butterfly Messenger will keep their secrets safe
Stars fall from the heavens one by one blessing their wishes created by Love ~JDR ♥

Chele Hummingbird

As the day go by and you're not near
Down my cheek falls a special tear
One by one down they fall
These silent tears break through my wall
I try so hard to be tough and strong
... to fight the tears until they're gone
In my heart there's an empty space
waiting for you to take its place
Forever I'll wait till you're by my side
But the pain I'm feeling I just can't hide
Give me your love ~ show me you care
Help me make it through this nightmare
Give me your hand and I'll give you mine
Together we'll fly to the end of time
The days without you seem like years
so I send these words with all my
silent tears.........

Chele Hummingbird

The blood that flows through you....
flows through me
when I look in any mirror
it's your face that I see
Take my hand
... lean on me
We're almost free
wandering soul...

Jude Joneson

You left me behind
Took everything else in your life to a new level
leaving importance behind
leaving fate behind, trust flew out the window
Love is shattered...
Friendship ties, lost forever...

Jude Joneson

Among the blue cascades of motionless clouds
I have found a new life
Mounds of black, red and brown sand encompass the mountain views
An azure blue lake marks the start of a new beginning
Love, peace and harmony, pleasure and humanity are now my focus
Happiness is now tenfold and desire is overwhelming
... Friends I met this week will be forever a part of my being...
Peace, patience and tranquillity have taken over my existence
To be and to be happy and to be pleasurable and peaceful is honourable
An infinity symbol now adorns my neck
I'm telling the world I am free to love and be happy...

Jude Joneson

Sitting here I have cried my eyes out
Day after day for the past eight months
Depression and anxiety have taken a toll on my weak focus of life
I wonder how my medication is helping me?
I ponder how I got to this point in my life....
At this point the eight months have become only a day...a major blur
I cry and stay at home, afraid to be happy, afraid to love
Feeling my life beginning to crumble more and more...
Afraid that my life will suddenly end and no one will care

Jude Joneson
Just a Love letter....

Thank you for the comfortable conversations, no matter how slowly or at what distance our courtship developed. I know standing before God and our future family, vowing to be your partner for life, was the easiest decision I have ever made

You have the greatest soul, the noblest nature, the sweetest, most loving heart I have ever known, and my love and admiration for you have increased so much since we've known each other that it still amazes me

... You are more wonderful and handsome in my eyes than you were before; and my pride and joy and gratitude that you should love me with such a perfect love are beyond all expression

Each day that passes makes over love for each other grow stronger. Although I know it's hard for us to be apart. I know, there is nothing that can keep us apart forever. Our desires will continue to stretch across any distance, over every mountain and ocean between us. Nothing can stand between us, and nothing will stop me from meeting you

you are my future and nothing can ever keep us from our destiny. I miss you more every day. I am here with open arms where you will someday finally arrive...right where you belong. If only I could have come up with the right words to describe the depth of this beautiful feeling that I have for you. I would have whispered them to you the first time we met. The best thing I can do is to show you now

I love you so much, sweetie. You are the best thing that ever happened to me. You are like the best poetry ever composed, the best song ever played, the best picture ever painted. I never thought someone like me could get so lucky

I love you more than my life, more than my world. I love you more and more each day and that is the most wonderful feeling any one can ever hope to experience

I hope to grow old with you for the rest of my life; to celebrate good times with you and support each other through the bad times. Marriage is a journey that we will grow together through. We will learn things about each other every day. We will not always have good times but we will always love each other and work through our problems. Marriage is forever. So I promise you forever. We will have fun watching football games, taking walks and watching movies. I look forward to that day and until then; I will be waiting for you with open arms and my heart full of love just for you.

Jude Joneson

Through the darkness I can see your light and you will always shine
I can feel your heart in mine
Your face I've memorized and I idolize just you
There is peace in my soul
For such a long awaited time
... There is love in my life
A love of melody and rhyme
Once you took hold of my heart
I knew no other could have reached
As whispered fate took my hand
To levels only you could reach.

You in my life
Will live eternally
I knew the first night we met
you were meant for me
I don't know how to say this

The words walking through my mind
I can't put pen to paper,
the sentence I can't find,
for the feelings deep inside my heart
I pray to God above
for the right words to tell you,
how much I have fallen in love
As I sit here and daydream
Of the first day we met
I can still see your eyes gleam
And I feel as if I won a bet
You're mine to keep
For now and forever
I love you with all my heart,
Our love is so deep
It's as if we are a piece of art
So I'm yours and you are mine

Jessica DayRodriguez

Before Me -

As my Mother and Father created me in love I know
May be this is not your story, but pieces if it can be learned from
Seeing aspects of yourself evolutionarily exposed as your ancestors
strives to see just as you focus your third eye on what is yet to be
But they only saw parts of a generation in bloom
Wanting so much more as their children grew
Two worlds collide literally, as my Mother the Goddess of Egyptian times and
my Father, one of the Indian spiritual minds
Their love was pure as every drop from the vast ocean and how they
met is such a dream if only to create me to be something
I didn't know quite how to grasp
As I lay in the embryo position within a womb that shelters me
the sense of the sun and moon's astrological
hold is as intense as my first breath

Knocked against my back in a slight
upside down position to breathe

In that moment I was awakened by all that came to be
Just me, already dying with each new breath
As my third eye no longer shown to the outside
Perceived only by me as a directional guild stronger than my heart, mind and
soul in one would ever be
Alone I survive just as before me

Mlungisi Makhanya

IN THE MIDDLE OF THE NIGHT
A CREWLING NOISE CLOSING UP TO MY PLACE OF BEAUTY SLEEP

LISTENING WITH BATED BREATH
WONDERING IF IT IS TIME
YOU CRAWL FROM THE FEET STRAIGHT UP
BRING THE SHIVER TO THE ALREADY SHIVERING MASS OF BLOOD...

Serpent Seven

Hey, that tickles
Yeah, right there
No point in staring
I don't mind that we're a pair
You know me better than anyone
I know you like a son
And you treat me better than the average fun
You're so good to me, so I don't bear to care
Who said the world was ever, really, quite fair

With notebook in hand, I find a wooded lot
I drag myself to a secluded spot
There, I sit, and just listen
There I sit, and smell
With eyes closed, I touch the bark on the trees
Picking clovers, and dandelions
Then, it happens, it's magical, unlike any orgasm before

My book opens and words flourish from nature store
Feelings, thoughts, expressions pour onto my pages
I collapse in exhaustion, crying and thankful
I give back to mother earth, from my body, my own fluids
Then, I return home, re-newed, re-born... Re-lived

Serpent Seven

Sleeping, sleeping and waking
I love them both, for different reasons
You make them both, filled with joy, and fear

Sleeping... To close my eyes and know your near
Waking... To open them slowly, and be your fears

No one has ever been this close
No one would ever make this choice
So I consider myself a lucky girl
And you're the only one for me in this world!
So here I stay, and lay with you dear
Sleeping, sleeping and waking, filled with joy, and fear
How did I get here? No worries, no fears. You fondle my breast, as I kiss your chest
You know me very well, my knees bend, I pass your navel. I undo your pants, like a South
American dance. You palm my head, as I pull out your pen. And with one thrust, I accept it,
past my tongue
It hurts my throat, but I like when it melts in my hands, so I stay true to the game, it's really
just a little pain
I cry like a bitch, and begin to twitch. All that doesn't help my now, my eyes water and I feel
so proud! My reward is near. I can smell it, I can taste it, and you begin to quiver
Now I'm in control, as you violently shake, no way on earth I'm letting go! My
encouragement for nourishment brings you to joy, as I make wet circles around your toy
All is over, all is done. I let you be, what magical fun

Serpent Seven

Tit for tat! I want to see them all
Don't be shy it's me
You and these four walls
You promised, so don't back out now
I have no problems undoing my paisley blouse
You go first, I'm revealing the worst
Your wife hates me, and my physical curse
But all that really matters is you seem to grow
When I accidentally brush up on you bro
Don't worry; I've noticed when you try to hide your opus
You got an hour before you have to go home
And I make that hour; powerful
Down to your bone

Serpent Seven

Get me high first, so I don't feel you inside my purse
Rummaging, breaking taking what is yours
Using my body as your open door
I brace myself, no cry for help
I'm a big girl now, with a big girl smile
You break right through to my inner core

No shame in your game
You use me like a puppet whore
I have no problem being your Muppet swore
And when you're done, you leave me like a slut Hun
Home to your wife, I know the priority game
I wonder, I wonder does she feel the same pain?

Molly Maharaj

Bird of every hue, Clouds in the sky so blue
Crisp breeze against your skin
Mountains rolling as far as the eye can see over valley's green
Flowers bright far n wide, friendly people laughing n smiling dancing
In the land God so abundantly blessed...South Africa

Thecla Shozi

Saw a smile fading away from her face!!!
Saw her brown face without a smile!!!
Her eyes bloodshot with pains
Tears rolling and falling in patters like rain!!!
Her hear dripping buckets of sorrow!!!
All her marital bliss turned a horrow!!!
Her brown creased into countless furrows!!!
D ever-recurring prints of blatantly brutal arrows from d one
She ever loved, d one she will 4rever love!!!
Still no sound of cry she gave!!!
All she did was gape at d bubbly chubby little one at play...
D fruit of her once sweet love!!!
Now it was all over d bubbles had all deserted d foam...
AGAIN SHE REACHED FOR THE BATTLE...
With a trance she took a swing from it!!!
This way was d only way for her, to win the battle o may so she thought!!!

Molly Maharaj

The Sound of Silence (written for interclass poetry '12)
By Atul Philipose on Friday, March 9, 2012 at 6:59pm ·
I made my way out of Kankanady station
Formal clothes in my bag, it was the end of vacation
Expecting academic robots for friends
Expecting the sound of silence

A rudely overpriced trip to Lalbagh later
The surprise awaiting me grew even greater
I found my kind, not robots but eager friends
They kept me from the sound of silence

The months that followed are supposedly manly
Alcohol and herbs, even with strangers Richard and Stanley
The promised daily calls to mom went for a toss and hence
She got accustomed to my sound of silence

First year, sitting in a crowd of two hundred and fifty
We were a threat to professors, most mean and hefty
Perhaps only for the last few minutes of attendance
Did they hear, the sound of silence

Second year was for exploring places far and wide
Sheep brain and pig intestine, all fancy food i tried
For cosmesis,i changed from glasses to contact lens
Fearing the sound of feminine silence

Football was initially a tactful venture
A golden chance to miss a boring lecture
Soon our success all over made us so-called "legends"
Medals broke through the sounds of silence

Applauding crowds, rousing ovation
Convention centre was my arena for creative demonstration
Even the Dean wanted a private audience
Far were the sounds of silence

Internship was to be the fulfilment of a dream
The first guy to approach a patient, I was now part of the team
On a tired evening, when an anxious patient spoke a word in excess
I blessed him with a frown, and the sound of silence

I bid goodbye to a friend at noon
I'm assured; I won't see him anytime soon
And now when it's time for me to jump the KMC fence
I've come to appreciate the sound of silence

What happens next I do not know
Despair tugs at my heart, it just won't go
I'll tell myself to hope and strive for excellence

Listening intently, my new found friend, the sound of silence

By Atul Philpose

Molly Maharaj

Let go of Sorrows
Let go of Pain
Let go of everything that may have hurt you to pain
Today is a New Day
Make your pain a foundation and love

Your only gain
Wishing u loving hearts darling Valentines...everywhere

AmaTainted Titles
From the back of the house
She could hear him yell
Cussing her and calling her a liar
It did not bother her any but she wished to set him straight...
His words quieted as she walked down the long corridor, her heeled foot sets,
drowning out his discontent...

"Liar?' she questioned as she reached his chambers, "...how so?"
"LOOK AT ME!!!" head jolts up, struggling in her bed. "You said..." he snarls and
grunts, through clenched teeth... the rage in his eyes fierce and downright sexy!
She smiles as she shakes her head... "I said...?" she teased.
"Ahh, yes... yes I did..." she sits on the bed at his side."I told you id love you
unconditionally, without constraints..." then she rises, places a tender kiss on his
cheek and turns to walk towards the door.

"Oh..." she turned to face him, "I didn't lie... I said 'constraints' at no time did I say,
'no restraints'..."
For measure, she checked the ties fastening him to the bed and for purpose, sucks
him unconscious.
"Really wish i could control my urges but you are just too damn desirable to resist at
times..." she wipes her mouth.
He awakes to darkness... senses alive to touch and sound and he asks, "are you still
here...?"
And you know i am... my perfume fills your nostrils as you breath in.
"Ama?" he begs her response
But she says nothing as she runs her soft finger over his toes and up his long,
muscular leg...
Leaving in the wake, tiny thrill bumps.
Leaning over his naked body, she attempts to blow life back into him but drained, he
remains flaccid,
Only soft moans stir in the air.
"I wish I knew the words to move you..." she sighed,
"I wish I had the touch that would excite you..."
In silence she sat, looking over his beautiful form. He too, was without words and his
face scrunched up in displeasure.
Time ticked away turning day shadows into nights gloom. his breaths slowing to
slight snores.
Faint whispers of "I'm sorry" go unheard and she set him free from the bindings,
Thinking it would be a fate worse than death,
That if in the mornings light, he would be gone from her bed
But she leaves him to sleep, wandering down the hall to the sofa,
Where she too, could find some rest.
However, seeking such comfort was in vain...
With every odd noise that creeked through the house, her eyes widened, afraid to
see him sneaking out...
But it was the chilled night air that woke her lastly...
Low clouds moved in through open windows...

Kissing her soft skin with dew
Rousing her stillness
And she thought of him:
Still sleeping,
Still bare,
Still beautifully sprawled out across the bed

Hunger urged her to returned to him
Though her haste was for not...
All that was left, were the crumpled sheets
And displaced pillows

Serpent Seven

If I lay here, perfectly still, could you resist my bonded wrists?
Wrapped ever so gently, and painted with your smile
No you see me giggle
From the three velvet kisses placed delicately on my emotional pile
Can you resist?

Serpent Seven

There's a storm coming, and it's painted with your kiss
As you moisten upon my troubled lips
Truth, as it is so delicately put,
It's going to hurt like an unforeseen hoof
Your complexion, as it turns from happy, to sad, to mad
I'll take my punishment as you rip me plaid
This will be our last poke, as you push me, I fall,
Head-first into the snow you can't live with what I just said
You can't live without my agony head
Snowflakes glistening in the winter sun are blinding me
as I walk towards the empty field
As I walk I notice little patterns of paw prints in the path
One large footprint catches my eyes
My throat jumps into my stomach not knowing what to do

Serpent Seven

Heaven must be here...
Bathed in flesh, blood, and bone
She stands before me with a smile of dandelions

And a body of a big bowl of cherries
When our lips touch, lavender, butterflies flutter,
Pink pebbles, pelts my arm and hands
I release just a little more as I'm adorned
And then, a return to earth
My soil irrigates to nurture your seeds

Jude Joneson

Walking down the road now....
DREAMS
DESIRES
Moving on with my life
Thinking I'm awakening from an era of cloudy existence...
KNOWING
Skipping merrily now....

Jude Joneson

You left me behind
Took everything else in your life to a new level
Leaving importance behind
Leaving fate behind, trust flew out the window
Love is shattered...
Friendship ties, lost forever...

Jessica DayRodriguez

Love Letter -

Since I practically live within walls of our diverse dilemmas
And the real beauty it creates between
Everyday missing your words
All of our shades new
At an unexpected open door, to individual
Journey; inspired by the awakened relationship we link precious.
Our dedicated experience each brings a sense of wonder.
Still always there is love... though now separate it will endure.
For as we once held hands and whispered in the dark; the difference

Being we now will look to the moon and stars to remind us of each other.
My only wish is for your happiness and success in life because
That is the only way I know to part. And even though we couldn't see
Through our promises made to one another, I do hope you find what
You're searching for within another's heart
We share a piece of each
Other that can never be taken away and I will cherish that the moment
Was with you every day
All my life, my dear
Never to fade

Jessica DayRodriguez

The Psychiatrist -

Meddling into someone's ideas...
That's an attempt to know the terrestrial, sometimes
Detrimental plunge of perception you studied because
You think you're not like the rest
How sublimating that world might be.
As you listen, or do you really hear?
Will you become their puppet for show?
Question for once your theories and daily planner
You had assigned. Wondered the reasons really?
Or do you entrust your sometimes passively sullen mind
Another's hell of wonders to escape one more time
"Excuse me... but it's past my time, can I go?" as
The patient exits the door

Resentment
By Tragedy L. Dark, TLD

I gave you an out, you choose to stay in
Now I`m wondering if you made the right choice to begin with
A person unable to see pass the past will never see the bright future ahead
I admit I've made wrong choices and occasionally been the fool
But under no circumstances was that your cue to be rude
Strong to the world but for you I was broken, battered, and weak I was definitely
yours but you made no attempt to keep

When I had enough realizing my heart had failed me for the last time
I was willing to allow it
I walked away defeated had down
White flag drawn and you convinced me to stay
Truth is you weren't sure how to love me
Or if you could love me, you just didn't want anybody else to love me
My complaints, my pleas and cries fell on selectively hearing deaf ears
Other saw heard them and wanted to be there
My resentment builds higher and higher
Because you were the only one I wanted to care
Resentment because you had an out stayed in but it never felt like you were near

Jaimal Anand
EVERY SUNRISE AND EVERY SUNSET
With every sunrise and sunset, there are a series of events
That unfold that we call our day, the events that unfold have,
In my view, two characteristics, one we can never reverse those events,
And two the events are surprises that either embrace us with warmth and care
Or bombard us like rockets

With every sunrise and sunset, we have choices
We can choose to allow these events destabilise us
Or we can choose to welcome each event, good and bad
What is our daily choice...do we really know what to do with the unknown....
Living is just a constant surprise,
And we react to those surprises with actions
That we cannot change ....nor can we?

Every sunrise and every sunset.....
Brings actions, every action creates events,
All these events put together we call our lives...or is it?

Porsche Honeycomb Tswina

Ultimately
Black hair turns white
Smile so bright risks tears
Junk food is good for your soul but will damage your heart
Crossing the street gets you a taxi, who knows?
In the end
Birth brings life
Hard work provides
Darling! Everything is a risk
You can never be too careful cause
Ultimately...you will!

Victor Lehlohonolo Nchabeng
Later

Later time to tell stories
Stories of Deceived Nation
Civilization was worth nothing
Pay no Attention and Regret Later

Sapphire Moon

A thought of creative energy flows through the winds of time
With each meeting of choices is a chance to look beyond
Now the door of light is open for all who look inside to dream
Wonder & invision for those who choose not to hide
By all of us seeking knowledge & the truths within
A healing process started when we adhered to love
It's a steady way of thinking to clear one's cluttered mind
In letting grace & mercy to never fall behind

Serpent Seven
Had an incredible weekend!
Saturday, I Drove to Ft. Washington Park
No radio, no cell phone, just me,
a few of my favourite pens and a brand new notebook
It was such a warm and inspiring day
I retracted my convertible top and began to write
I wrote about me, you, and all the things I wanna do
I wrote about the moon and stars; my emotional spawns
Past and present falls
I wrote about lace panties and a matching bra
Even my uncontrollable walls

And then for an instant that lasted for hours I was in awe, I felt its power
It was orgasmic, and tickled a little
Almost like god playing her fetus fiddle
Getting dark I awoke out of my trance
Walked into the woods and opened my hands
I dug a whole not far in the ground and buried my notebook
And pen without sound
What I wrote came from earth; I returned my blessings to comfort her
I took the back roads home Saturday night

Serpent Seven
Wanna share a secret?
Painted with your smile
Me, and you and my emotional dial
Just spin my wheel, and I'll laugh, cry or kneel
Your heaven on earth, and I wanna cop-a-feel!

Mlungisi Makhanya
SEAS SEE THE FISH
YOU BOO WANTS TISH
Y CHEAT WANNA TEACH
ME SOME LESSON
YOU ONLY LESSEN
YOURSELF
BETTER HIDE IN THE SHELF
YOU DON`T CHERISH
WHAT U GOT U ONLY WANT SHERIF
YOU ARE OUT OF CONTROL
IF U THINK U HAVE IT ALL
I SAW U WITH A NURSE
ONE WITH A NASTY ASS
WHAT TO SAY FOR YOSELF?
ONLY WANTED A FUCK INSTEAD OF A DUCK

Demetria HotChocolate Fails

Take a Moment

The journey of man along life's history
Some bathe in sweat n grime while other's on silken spreads
Is the journey of learnin`, of lovin` n livin` of hatin` n forgivin`
Some are harder, some too long yet some that seem to end too fast

Whatever your journey, whatever the place
Remember that ultimately it's between your Maker n U

Demetria HotChocolate Fails

There's a light at the end of the tunnel but i'm gonna have to fight my way out of it and I hope you'll
be waiting at the end for me. I was fighting to get to you in the end. ♥

Demetria HotChocolate Fails

I long for the day to kiss your lips
To feel your breath
To feel you arms wrap around me like a straightjacket
To listen to your heart beat like a beautiful beat to a great song in my ear

Demetria HotChocolate Fails

He makes my heart skip a beat or two
Quite funny but true
Just listening to him laugh makes me smile for a little while
What makes him special?
His carefree spirit, his laid back charm
a joke that he doesn't have to work too hard to make me laugh at♥

Thecla Shozi

I'll Give You, Your Space In my Heart
Some say South Africa is a dark continent
Some said year 2000 was the world end
Some even says HIV/AIDS is the end of life
If there is any truth to this we shall see the bunch of pigs flying
No matter whom you are
What you are, where you are
Don't worry about anything
You have my love, my support n treatment to keep you going
I'll never abandon you just because you have this nasty HIV
I'll give you, your space in my heart
Who said it is an ultimate punishment?
No One!!!
If it was so; then what?
What about those innocent young girls and boys?
What sin have they committed to deserve such pain in their heart?
I'll be there when those uneducated people harass you

And I will be gently to you like a dove
You are a human, you feel like one
You are at home to me
You can chat n laugh with us
Don't worry about anything
I will give you, your space in my heart
Burst and cry your anger our it's okay
But stressing about it, it only steal your life away
AIDS has no authority or the power to break that intended bond
Respective community we should stand for our people all the way
The time has come to reveal our true colours
With God's willing we will get out of these shackles of AIDS
Africans shall lead the way
We have survived so many before
How dare we should doubt ourselves now?

Sherry Weaver

"Darkness inside my head"
When I see them all around
I can't believe what I found,
I found the way to visit-
Even when they're dead
I found them in a little room-
Locked inside my head.,
When I opened up that door
I saw the ones, who lived no more,
I saw their fate, their deep abyss-
I saw the ones, - I truly missed.,
I came across a place for me,
Where death is truly life,
I found it, the place to see
All the death and broken dreams,
All the darkness and tragedies,
All that passed before my eyes.
Even here in my head
It's full of pain, mixed with dread,
My lifeless soul, now dark and dead

Jude Joneson

Falling
As we meet again and again
I fall more freely, without restraint
Trying to catch myself
To slow the descent
To no avail, I remain to fall, still further
It's so exhilarating
To fall so freely, defying those who say
Beware!
Hopefully, my chute will open
Before it's too late
For I know the ground is down there somewhere
Sitting here I have cried my eyes out day after day for the past eight months
Depression and anxiety has taken a toll on my weak focus of life
I wonder how my medication is helping me
I ponder how I got to this point in my life
At this point the eight months have become only a day...a major blur
I cry and stay at home, afraid to be happy... afraid to love
Feeling my life beginning to crumble more and more...
Afraid that my life will suddenly end and no one will care

Jessica DayRodriguez

Simply You –

I dreamed there would
Be a better tomorrow
Then you came into my life & you've
Taken away all my sorrow
My days of sad are thing
Of my past
Because...I have found
Love at last!
My days of emptiness
Are gone for good
Because you fill a void in
My heart that I had a feeling you would...

You've opened a window
You've shown me a light
And my love for you will...
Continue to burn bright... JDR

Serpent Seven

Oh where, oh where did my angel go?

Maybe across town, maybe to, and fro
Maybe she's somewhere picking dandelions for her hair
Maybe she's in an alley making out with bear?
I really don't know, but my halo broke
And I'm provoked to host my throat
Oh where, oh where, did my angel go?

Serpent Seven

You bested me. I am no longer just one
When the dust settles I'd even bare you a son
For 21 years I've lived alone, and now my love involves you Hun
I use to only do for me
My selfish ways, my insecurities, but now it's true
I'm blue without my boo It's you, for truth, my mystery sloth

Molly Maharaj

From my heart to yours
A year is almost over,
A journey lost in time
Dreams lost and found
A time to take a moment to recall promises made
A time to pick the broken pieces and mend roads long forgotten
Nobody knows what tomorrow holds
Nobody knows if they'll wake to see the new dawn
But today is here, with memories shared, and hopes to make anew the scars of yesteryear
These lines I write for the ones like me
Who wonder still in the hope to find the answers yet not found
the seasons not yet enjoyed, the dreams still not made real
People my people far and wide...on this journey in time
I love u all...God bless u on your journey :)

Porsche Honeycomb Tswina
No! No! no! Am not gonna be poetic about the ending year
Can I be soulistic then? Of course!
Looking back in the year, I have grown
Not only as a person but in every way
Spiritually, I am closer to my God
My faith has been tested and I can say is stronger
I have yet been blessed with a job I love
God is still good
Yes there are times when I felt He had forsaken me
Yet He emerged as the Victor! I am grateful
Professionally, I am at a stage where I can say I am recognised
I am one of the young women in politics

and I am making a contribution in changing people's lives
I am pleased with my progress

Personally...it's been a journey!
I have gotten rid of some habits
Been through hell!
It hasn't been an easy year for me
And the scars will take longer to heal
But the person I am is stronger and wiser
I have grown.
What I have learnt though is that

The values one is brought up on
Is the cornerstone of life
The decisions we make are influenced by them
Love, respect, humbleness, humility, giving,
Honesty and fear of God are what make you a person
I have grown...

Serpent Seven
You never cease to amaze,
How you craze me
Through mind, body
My soul has no choice but to follow
Like a slave to its master
I'm captured
Your tongue is the most powerful persuader
You bring me mountains of gushy-lust with each thrust
And true favours
No girl's dignity is braver
During the day I savoured
What became of me last night and my behaviour?
What becomes of me tonight?
Not even god's favours in site
What you do to me
So I'm here on all fours
Begging to be your sore whore
Well you bate me? Will you take me?
Only the wind knows as it blows
And I wait for my fate on your floor

Serpent Seven

Make me stay for it
Make me pray for it
Bound tight in this swing
Masked and waiting on you to bring me pleasure
Whenever you decide to come
What fun when twirled and spun

Serpent Seven
MY LAST MOMENTS
You cling to my breast, like a well nourished newborn
Licking and sucking my life's essence for your very, selfish, and own
You always have, and always will; I know that now
And time never stands still, but it doesn't really matter to me
I'd give you my air, for you to breathe
As I wilt away, you grow stronger
Filling yourself with my dignity and honour
I happily, and with open arm release my life into your palms
My reasons for living have never meant so little
As I close my eyes upon your pillow
You smile as I try to gather what's left
I cling to you as I slowly accept death

Serpent Seven
Most of my muse is bits and pieces of previous writings of done
Experiences, feelings, and personal emotions (in that order) seem to be my basis
Somehow, they just all seem to come out/back when I write
It pulls out of me right onto the paper so I don't go and do something foolish or stupid
A release or outlet if you will; necessary, mental, climatic, moments in my short life
Often I find myself holding back or not totally forthcoming when I write on FB
I have been threatened, followed, stalked, ridiculed, labelled a devil worshiper
And once an attempted exorcism by a so-called on-line priest!
For me, writing is really about a journey back to what's real
Or what is considered reality here, here in society
I often, cognitively, and slowly/daily get into these states of blankness, or unreal/unrest
and it wreaks havoc on my personal and professional life
Writing lets me bridge the gap safely between my realities and my mind
If I didn't write, they would blur, or mix violently, and eventually consume me with them
LOL, an exorcism wouldn't be too far off the mark then...
So for me writing is necessary for survival
I have known this for a long time and embrace it
However I haven't championed it yet
That is my personal goal for me
So, until then, here I am, bleeding and writing, for all to see and read

Serpent Seven

You move my hair, as you stare and I R.E.M. away on an island, far
Just me, you and the stars, holding hands by day, fishing by night
No clock to chain to
No boss to fight
My heart floats in-between your arms
Laughing from one-liners and all of your charms
And then I wake to find you not there
By my lonesome, not strong enough to bare
I weep god's prayer seven fold. You never reveal yourself, truth be told

Serpent Seven

Your here for me again, an eventful, rapist, trend. I'm young and innocent; you greet me as a friend. Quick to see, I'm just another mare for you to share. You split me to my core, I scream as a breathe; you treat me as a whore. I grin and I bare it. Afterwards, you kiss my head, and tear it. I'm shaking and bleeding from cardinal sin, you don't spare it. You spit on me, and laugh, brash as you butcher it. I cry out in a deafening, silent sound. And I thought you'd marry it

Serpent Seven

Magnificent man in a pan, with a spray on tan. No FAM, no ham. Just himself and his hands. How selfish you are, by your own drinks at the bar. I don't need a man with a tan. I have my own lovely, soft, moisten, hands!

Serpent Seven

Today, I remember... To be thankful for what? On that dreaded day, you washed my family away. My Father pushed me to higher ground as he drowned. My Mother was swept away, her body later found. Why god did you spare me? We god do you watch me bleed. So here a lay, no arms to pray. No legs to walk. I'll just slither away. Out of your body, out of your light. No thanks again, from you tonight...

Mlungisi Makhanya
CAN YOU HEAR ME SPEAK?

I ASK NOT TO CHANGE YOURSELF

IF U DO, DO IT FOR YOURSELF
I ASK NOT FOR MIRACLES
I ONLY NEED A FRIEND
SOMEONE TO CRACKLE
JOKES WHEN I AM WITH
I ASK NOT FOR U TO BE CLEVER
I NEED YOU AS YOU ARE
I DONT NEED WITTY BRAINS

I JUST NEED A FRIEND
TO LISTEN TO ME
TO SHARE THEIR JOY & PAIN
I AM YOUR GIVEN SOUL
USE ME DONT ABUSE ME
I PROMISE NO HEAVEN NOR HELL
I JUST WANT YOUR BOSSOM
TO LIE ON YOUR CHEST
LISTEN TO YOUR MELODICAL VOICE

I ASK NOT 4 U TO COMPROMISE YOSELF
JUST BE THERE LOOKING AFTER MEI PROMISE TO LOOK AFTER YOU
I ASK NO GOLD OF YOU
I ALREADY HAVE DA PLATINUM
CAN U DO ME ONE FAVOUR
LIVE YOUR DREAM FOR YOURSELF
IF U DO I WILL BE ABLE TO IT MYSELF
I ASK NOT FOR YOUR PAIN
I NEED TO SEE YOU HAPPY
LIVE AND LET LIVE
LOVE THY NEXT PERSON
AS MUCH U DO U

IF YOU CAN DREAM, DREAM BIG
DONT FAIL YOUR DREAMS FOR ME
IF YOU CAN PULL ME UP
PLEASE DO IT WITHOUT PAIN
IF YOU CAN BE HAPPY FOR U
DO IT SO I CAN BE HAPPY TOO

LOVE IS 4 DA GIVEN!

Molly Maharaj

Journey of Life

Long ago when we were young

We played a dare just for fun
We laughed n loved mostly for fun
The consequences meant no harm

Time has passed
Our lives have stretched
Across the land n seas afar
Leaving paths of broken dreams n tears

The journey seemed to never end
But day by day it got further
Some cut short by the hands of fate
Some to reach another pace

To my family n friends far n wide
Thank u 4 sharing this life with me
For adding colour n flavour to this dream
That we share this day 4ever

NOBANTU NGONTSHANE
LOVE WHICH YOU NEVER TOUCH
Missing you is something I hate most in my life
I must forget the past and focus on the present
Some joys are best celebrated in silence than laughter
Though I never met you our chats have grown in me
Your chats are inside my skin
Going to sleep having not chatted with you
Is like going to bed without food
Though friends ask if I enjoy a relationship with you
I say a big yes because I have a bigger picture of you in my heart

You mean the world to me
Having not spoken with makes me lose it
My love for you is real and you mean the world to me
I love you not for who you are but for what I am
When I chat with you
Thanks for being a part of my life
And especially for making me find out who I am
I follow my heart as I hold you close to heart
You are my heart, soul, my universe and everything
Never will I ever give up on us
We may not be together right now, but, we will be someday

With your words you brighten my past and present
As such I pray to God to brighten our future together forever and ever
My heart is hot with passion and I'm ignited by a spark of desire
The flame of love bring about rosy smokes
Love is full of roads, as we travel we try to forget some
Some we wish never passed
As much as there are many thousands of obstacles on our way
There is only one reason why you are my love
You are not only my truelove; you are my soul mate and my everything

Acceptance develops one's ability to change and adapt
So there is a shift from the past to the present
Our feelings are our tool to bring us together

Molly Maharaj

My Husband

Someone to love and someone to scold
Someone who's very much your own
He wills love u in the morning
And 4get u when it's noon
He will smile and pretend to listen
When your story u will tell

But my husband is my strength
Who will love me when I'm old
And see me as the one he met
Long time ago

He'll often drive u crazy
And you'll swear he was by the demon possessed
He'll even make u feel
Moments of terrible anxiety

But my husband he is,
One long chosen 4 me
And so will remain,
Until eternity

Jessica DayRodriguez

Before Me -

As my Mother and Father created me in love I know
Maybe this is not your story, but pieces if it can be learned from
Seeing aspects of yourself evolutionarily exposed as your ancestors
Strives to see just as you focus your third eye on what is yet to be
But they only saw parts of a generation in bloom
Wanting so much more as their children grew
Two worlds collide literally, as my Mother the Goddess of Egyptian times and my Father
One of the Indian spiritual minds
Their love was pure as every drop from the vast ocean
And how they met is such a dream if only to create me to be something
I didn't know quite how to grasp
As I lay in the embryo position within a womb that shelters me
The sense of the sun and moon's astrological

Hold is as intense as my first breath
Knocked against my back in a slight
Upside down position to breathe, in that moment I was awakened by
All that came to be
Just me, already dying with each new breath
As my third eye no longer shown to the outside
Perceived only by me as a directional guild stronger than my heart, mind and
Soul in one would ever be.
Alone I survive just as before me

Molly Maharaj

Journey of Life

Long ago when we were young
We played a dare jus for fun
We laughed n loved mostly for fun
The consequences meant no harm

Time has passed
Our lives have stretched
Across the land n seas afar
Leaving paths of broken dreams n tears

The journey seemed to never end
But day by day it got further
Some cut short by the hands of fate
Some to reach another pace

To my family n friends far n wide
Thank u for sharing this life with me
For adding colour n flavour to this dream
That we share this day forever

Jude Joneson
My mother played piano
And I would dance
When our house caught fire
I mimicked the flames with the arch of my body
My mother stared solidly into the blaze
She leapt only once
When the piano peeled away from its legs
And twanged into a crackled chord
When the song ended

Curls of dust rose in adagio
And followed my lead
My spirit found its form in fire.
My dance ignited its sparks.

Now I spring past myself into your light
I am tour blink and your grasp
Your leap up from the kitchen table
The turn of your head to your lover's voice
My spirit is the static of her negligee
As the material clings

I cling and you are lit

Jude Joneson
Through the darkness, I can see your light and you will always shine
I can feel your heart in mine
Your face I've memorized and I idolize just you
There is peace in my soul
For such a long awaited time
There is love in my life
A love of melody and rhyme
Once you took hold of my heart
I knew no other could have reached
As whispered fate took my hand
To levels only you could reach
You in my life
Will live eternally
I knew the first night we met
You were meant for me
I don't know how to say this
The words walking through my mind
I can't put pen to paper
The sentence I can't find
For the feelings deep inside my heart
I pray to God above
For the right words to tell you
How much I have fallen in love
As I sit here and daydream
Of the first day we met
I can still see your eyes gleam
And I feel as if I won a bet
You're mine to keep
For now and forever
I love you with all my heart
Our love is so deep
It's as if we are a piece of art
So I'm yours and you are mine

73

Jude Joneson
Yesterday love was simple
Two lives sharing memories
Today it is more complicated
Starting over is scary and unsettling
Loving another makes me anxious and cautious
Love has always been love, yet can I return it?
Can I now accept it with no limitations?
Strangely, I feel taken advantage of.
Love has no boundaries or guarantees.
I am no longer interested in forever.
Passion sparks at inopportune moments
Waiting around makes me impatient and unyielding
Why has love become an unspoken word that is felt and not returned?
Was yesterday forever and can today be yesterday?

Jude Joneson

Darkness By: Jude Joneson 7-18-2011

Tempting

Seductively

Behave

Forces

Challenging

Voices

Be Wicked

Answering

Bravely

Memories

Choking

Aura

Fading

Throbbing

Listening

Whispering

Falling

Remembering

Screaming

Smouldering

Mlungisi Makhanya

Love one Another

The knowledge that God has loved me beyond all limits

Will compel me to go into the world

To love others in the same way

Love is spontaneous

But it has to be maintained through discipline ♥

L. Tsomo

SUNSET Balmy ruby shades, Attractive speechless sunlight

Dull vivid twilight!

FLOWERS sparkling blossoms, Reddish perfumed aroma!

GRASS Drowsy dews lay cold, a verdant clay carpet, a green earth scent

Molly Maharaj

Listen my friend, Listen to the cries

Of your brethren across the miles
Hark, they all sound the same
The cry of hunger, the cry of pain
Of unheard voices
Crying out in vain
When will we learn, When will we see
The painful pleas
Have no colour or creed

Serpent Seven

I am your marionette
Move my strings, and I'll dance for you
Whenever you want, I'm here for you
My permanent smile, my emotional pile
Play second best to your cognitive mile
I am your marionette!

Thecla Shozi
BE the Man
Be the man and sing along to the unwanted pleasures of two hands beating a drum!!!
Working simultaneously in melody, not making a song of love but one of lust...
So b d man and say your song, was a song of pain!!! Dedicated to me!!!
Be the man and write me a four page letter every time you hurt me with your heartless manly intentions...
That leads to my tears, which you burn and dry on my face...
Be the man that you are and cowardly admit your faults in figures of speech
In images of a more friendly nature
When you know that is not true
Talk dirty, beat me, strip my dignity and leave me bare...
And say we made love
Be the man and let me breath again,
Let me be same and claim freedom of an independent woman,
Let my happiness over yours, be relevant and let me be...
Be the man, regain your moralities and give yourself to the authorities...
Confess to being a...

Thecla Shozi

I'll Give You, Your Space In my Heart
Some say South Africa is a dark continent
Some said year 2000 was the world end
Some even say HIV/AIDS is the end of life
If there is any truth to this we shall see the bunch of pigs flying
No matter whom you are
What you are, where you are
Don't worry about anything
You have my love, my support n treatment to keep you going
I'll never abandon you just because you have this nasty HIV
I'll give you, your space in my heart
Who said it an ultimate punishment?
No One!!!
If it was so, then what?
What about those innocent young girls and boys?
What sin have they committed to deserve such pain in their heart?
I'll be there when those uneducated people harass you...
And I will b gently to you like a dove
You are a human, you feel like one,
You are at home to me,
You can chat n laugh with us,
Don't worry about anything!!!
I will give you, your space in my heart,
Burst n cry your anger our it's okay,
But stressing about it, it only steal your life away,
AIDS has no authority or the power to break that interned bond,
Respective community we should stand for our people all the way
The time has come to reveal our true colours
With God's willing we will get out of these shackles of AIDS
Africans shall lead the way
We have survived so many before
How dare we should doubt ourselves now?

Jaimal Anand
That point between dark and light, that twilight
That place...I like it...you may ask why
But for some of us we hurt others are forgiven
And go on living....victims live with that hurt for life
Who is selfish and who is honest...think I'm selfish

Kynthia I. Thisbe

"It is only with the heart that one can see a pure love; what is essential to the mind in these matters
is invisible to the eye. And words never spoken are as tainted as actions never followed through so
turned to lies. It's easier to respect when one is straight forward with which way they choose to turn
if dealing with you too; otherwise I wouldn't give a damn, if you want to follow a path to who knows
where the hell to" KIT

Kynthia I. Thisbe

"Should we confess all our mistakes to one another, if not just for the laughter it would cause for our lack of originality? Or would we for once see we are at times on the same road together even through our journey individually? I always question ways to bridge the gap so that we may be as a true "one love" someday in history long enough to be written in stone even if I am passed. For the children I will leave behind, my nieces and nephews, deserve to know I at least tried." KIT

Donna Osborn Clark

"Extraordinary is the "extra" that makes us more than ordinary. The "extra" that you have is your gift that will make you shine in HIS brilliant light once you share it with the world." ~ Donna Osborn Clark

Kynthia I. Thisbe

"To love with a shattered heart and fell many times to my knees if not further; yet still I will always reach for the stars, whatever happens -happens but not without a fight from within the depths of me." KIT

Sherry Weaver
"Darkness inside my head"
When I see them all around
I can't believe what I found,
I found the way to visit-
Even when they're dead
I found them in a little room-
Locked inside my head
When I opened up that door
I saw the ones, who lived no more,
I saw their fate, their deep abyss-
I saw the ones, - I truly missed
I came across a place for me,
Where death is truly life,
I found it, the place to see
All the death and broken dreams,
All the darkness and tragedies,
All that passed before my eyes.
Even here in my head
It's full of pain, mixed with dread,
My lifeless soul, now dark and dead

Molly Maharaj

A Cry in the Wild written 1997

The voice of Justice cries out in me
Break out of this Corruption fate we see
Make a statement show your stand
Sit not wondering what the plan is

General discussions and silent pleas
Can't make a future for you or me
We have a right in this world to be
We're not alone you will see

The road is long that's for sure
With many a turn and many a stone
But success has never in time been won
On wistful thinking and idle dreaming

Molly Maharaj

NOSTALGIA Nov. 1992

In the land of my forefathers alone I stand
With memories flashing by
Of day's n years I once lived
In a land that once bore me.

A wave within threatens to rise
And open flood gates that stand so dry
For want of reason to cry

But home is where I stand rite now
And here is where I must be
Fore 'tis but a passing phase
One long chosen for me

In all my years I've never known
A yearning such as this
For family lost n friends once known
And a land I may never see

Jessica DayRodriguez
Black Crow Blue -
The fever broke
But the other side of sickness would never know wellness truly

I didn't mean to but I became the kind of person that knows
Themselves so well that everyone else would remain a stranger
So to move like a worm under the earth without any need for eyes
Nothing to see just feel; feel all my hurt pleasuring at times
Gradually I watch it happen, seeds that become
Blades of grass poking out from the sand
Like the dirty needles plunged in my heart also creating the poison
That slips through my veins
All my loves are suicide and all my lovers a simple razor blade
Drink me now like a sweet aged glass of wine that love also ferments
The same way and grows more intoxicating day by day

Jaimal Anand

The mist in the forest is a strange phenomenon
Only if you been in a snowy sub zero alpine forest
You would know that feeling as armies once set up camp
Soldiers enduring the anxiety of the looming battle at dawn
The darkness only broken by the rays of the full moon
Shimmering through the thick of the wood
The smell in the air is a strange combination of the aroma of glory
And the stench of fear, armies throughout history has felt this
Jackals in the distance, the hoot of an owl, the whisper of the breeze through the trees-
Like life, waiting for the dawn, we feel fear
But the mild rays of moonlight sooth the grimness
Make the jackals sound less like an evil omen
And the hoot of an owl becomes comforting
Did I dream this last night?
I did...but I also remember my late night wintery walks and drives in those alpine mountains

Jaimal Anand

Just 3 questions

Is pain a sensation, a feeling or just a figment of our imagination, like fear or anxiety....?
Can we feel empathy or sympathy without knowing pain.....?
Are we just fools and slaves to our thoughts...?

Jude Joneson

Sitting on a bench waiting for a storm I feel love
I gaze in bewilderment as I notice

A star appears though the stormy clouds and is shining down on me
This is a star of hope
I am a child of the stars, age is timeless
I was put on Earth for a specific reason
It is my goal to help others realize they are also like me
Love and peace are my main focus
They will come back to Earth when we accept them
Than want us to live in peaceful tranquillity
Life and love are precious to them as it should be to us
We have the power to change all humanity, our destiny
When In doubt I look up and they are watching over me

Author Otis Randolf

Out of Habit

Some days I want to grab and shake you...
Just as a means to open your eyes
Look at yourself baby!!
You've been looking like that for a while
Where's the light in your eyes?
That brilliant brown colour is shrouded in depression
And... what about that bubbling personality?
That bright smile that illuminates any dark, dismal place

Help me understand what you're going through
The rough side of life has some smooth roads
But... from the wounds you seem to lick constantly
And the bruises on your heart and soul
Seems like you're struggling on the road alone
But your other half, cruises in their comfort zone
He laughs and smiles with everyone else around him
But barks and yells at you like a two dollar whore
Please... help me understand the love in your relationship

I know you love him... dedicated to him
But I can't help to think it's just out of habit
I'm sure he loves you... in his own way
But I can't help to think it's just out of habit
You turn to me for some peace in your world of thunder
But I wonder if that... is just out of habit
So if you are using me just out of habit
Then let me break this bad habit
I can't compromise our friendship of love and trust
Just because the events in your life... are just simply out of habit

Akhona Qabaka

Player got to retire
With poetry in my head and a pensile in my hand
Spitting vigorous sums of calculated and tested motionless poetry
Stand corrected being cool, calm and collected during the discussion we just completed
Let me flow and blow your mind
With fumes that will fumigate with a fragrance of love in your society
Or my poetry society
Fragrance of love that has infected and affected players
And those played by players or should I say lovers as we call them these days
Don't ask me how I know these things
I was a player before I got injured in the mid section
I said got injured in the mid section now I cannot run nor could I hide
Waist down waist up I have wasted my time on worthless things
Like running behind them skirts eKasi calling myself NBP a Natural Born Player
Life of a player is exciting, trilling, fulfilling yet dangerous so you need to man up and keep fit
I have been running, dodging, ducking everything in my way just to survive a bit
I have been ducking bullets running for cover for I was under her covers in the bedroom
That belong to another covered story that I won't uncover
I've been dodging babes shooting towards my direction asking "Are you my daddy"?
Off cause I'm not your daddy but you look like that girl that almost got me killed last year
Now I'm leaving the game behind
Oh wait take these condoms I don't need to have
Or hide them in my pocket and wallet
I don't need them anymore
They say players change but the game remains the same
Not true the game has change and players multiplied
I feel the game aint safe no more
That's why I have to leave the game
I used to sing while I swung them hips in my grille locked under the blankets of sinful love
Sin full love, coz I have seen you full of love so
I seized the moment to fulfil your desires of sinful love
I call it sinful love coz I left you out of love
Slowly I'm slipping and sliding away from all these things
I'm tired of waiting for change I decided to be the change
And raise my white flags saying I surrender my everything to you
Before I get HIV Accept me just as I am coz there's no other
I better rewrite my destiny and clean my eyes
My eyes have been blinded by the blistering passion
That has blasted many of us with ideas of love and love making
How can you make something that you can't even see?
So much for love!
Hayi ndiyahamba ndikhululeni to take my new life as a coach

Coaching players wanna bees about the life of a player
Life aint what it seem to be, used to be
Life has taught one thing if you aint got it go seek it
I'm waiting for people to sign up here's your chance come seek it

Author Otis Randolf

I Squandered My Soul Last Night

I squandered my soul last night
Trying to heal my broken heart
I miss the strength of security you seem to bring
When we are in one another's arms

I know I can't duplicate it
So why not be patient and wait for love again?
After all, love found me when I was ripe
Basking in heaven's light
Sweet enough to pick
And be replanted in that golden heart of yours

We sew good seeds

And harvested beautiful and delicious fruit
Joy rained down on us like they were God's own tear drops
And blessings were ours to claim for the goodness that flowed between us

But grace departed from us slowly
And you were no longer a part of me
I cried the memories from my mind
One tear at a time
And became the sacrificial lamb for others to devour

I squandered my soul last night.
Hoping I'd find peace that fled from me
When you turned and said, "so long" to me
I had to find that quiet strength
That kept me safe and warm at night

But the temporary fix... didn't last too long
And now I'm here like a junkie
Looking... for my next emotional high
I squandered my soul last night

Serpent Seven

How did I get here?
No worries, no fears
You fondle my breast, as I kiss your chest
You know me very well, my knees bend
I pass your navel
I undo your pants, like a South American dance
You palm my head, as I pull out your pen
And with one thrust, I accept it, past my tongue
It hurts my throat, but I like when it melts in my hands
so I stay true to the game; It's really just a little pain
I cry like a bitch, and begin to twitch
All that doesn't help me now, my eyes water and I feel so proud!
My reward is near; I can smell it, I can taste it, you begin to quiver
Now I'm in control, as you violently shake, no way on earth I'm letting go!
My encouragement for nourishment brings you to joy
As I make wet circles around your toy
All is over, all is done. I let you be, what magical fun

Serpent Seven

Tit for tat! I want to see them all
Don't be shy it's me, you, and these four walls
You promised, so don't back out now
I have no problems undoing my paisley blouse
You go first, I'm revealing the worst
Your wife hates me, and my physical curse
But all that really matters is you seem to grow
When I accidentally brush up on you bro
Don't worry; I've noticed when you try to hide your opus
You got an hour before you have to go home
And I'll make that hour; powerful
Down to your bone

Serpent Seven

Get me high first, so I don't feel you inside my purse
Rummaging, breaking
Taking what is yours
Using my body as your open door
I brace myself, no cry for help
I'm a big girl now, with a big girl smile
You break right through to my inner core
No shame in your game
You use me like a puppet whore
I have no problem being your Muppet swore
And when you're done, you leave me like a slut Hun
Home to your wife, I know the priority game
I wonder, I wonder does she feel the same pain

Molly Maharaj

Bird of every hue
Clouds in the sky so blue
Crisp breeze against your skin
Mountains rolling as far as the eye can see over valley's green
Flowers bright far n wide
Friendly people laughing n smiling
Dancing in the land God so abundantly blessed...South Africa
Molly Maharaj / Pinto

Thecla Shozi

Saw a smile fading away from her face!!! Saw her brown face without a smile!!! Her eyes bloodshot with pains, tears rolling and falling in patters like rain!!! Her hear dripping buckets of sorrow!!! All her marital bliss turned a horrow!!! Her brown creased into countless furrows!!! D ever-recurring prints of blatantly brutal arrows, frm d one She ever loved, d one she will 4rever love!!! Still no sound of cry she gave!!! All she did was gape at d bubbly chubby little one at play... D fruit of her once sweet love!!! Now it was all over d bubbles had all deserted d foam... AGAIN SHE REACHED FOR THE BATTLE... With an trance she took a swing frm it!!! Dis way was d only way for her, to win the battle o may so she thought!!!

Molly Maharaj

Let go of Sorrows, Lets go of Pain, Let go of everything that may have hurt you to pain

Today is a New Day, Make ur pain a foundation and luv ur only gain.

Wishing u luving hearts darling Valentines...everywhere :D

Serpent Seven

What are the answers, to the questions of me? Alone in a room, with 7 windows, and 3 doors. Shall I wake, or shall I sleep? Curled, comfortably upon hardwood floors. Listening to mother earth's heartbeat (pit-pat, pit pat). Listening in on soldiers stomped, feet (1-2-3, 1-2-3).

Serpent Seven

If I lay here, perfectly still, could you resist my bonded wrists? Wrapped ever so gently, and painted with your smile. No. You see me giggle. From the three velvet kisses, placed delicately, on my emotional pile. Can you resist?

Serpent Seven

There's a storm coming, and it's painted with your kiss
As you moisten upon my troubled lips
Truth, as it is so delicately put
It's going to hurt like an unforeseen hoof
Your complexion, as it turns from happy, to sad, to mad
I'll take my punishment as you rip me plaid
This will be our last poke
As you push me, I fall, head-first into the snow
You can't live with what I just said; you can't live without my agony head

Njabulo Preacher S Makhanya
Relationships are being tested
As the planet of discipline and maturity;
Leans on your heart strings
It means you're mixing with people of power and status
And walking away from anything that no longer works

Jude Joneson

Snowflakes glistening in the winter sun
Are blinding me as I walk towards the empty field
As I walk I notice little patterns of paw prints in the path
One large footprint catches my eyes
My throat jumps into my stomach not knowing what to do

Serpent Seven

Heaven must be here...
Bathed in flesh, blood, and bone
She stands before me with a smile of dandelions
And a body of a big bowl of cherries
When our lips touch, lavender, butterflies flutter
Pink pebbles, pelt my arm and hands
I release just a little more as I'm adorned
And then, a return to earth
My soil irrigates to nurture your seeds

Serpent Seven

Hey, I'm over here
Somewhere between god and your left ear
If you blink twice and smile real nice
I'll make sure I stay around
I love you, in a superficial way
My heart doesn't beat twice
In a month, or a day
So here we are, giggling up at the stars
Are backs laid on god's given earth, your hands in my bra?
Staring and dreaming, at what could become
You're staring, I'm dreaming of making you come

Serpent Seven

Had an incredible weekend!
Saturday, I Drove to Ft. Washington Park
No radio, no cell phone, just me, a few of my favourite pens
And a brand new notebook
It was such a warm and inspiring day
I retracted my convertible top and began to write
I wrote about me, you, and all the things I wanna do
I wrote about the moon and stars; my emotional spawns
Past and present falls, I wrote about lace panties and a matching bra
Even my uncontrollable walls
And then for an instant, that lasted for hours
I was in awe, I felt its power

It was orgasmic, and tickled a little
Almost like god playing her fetus fiddle
Getting dark I awoke out of my trance
And walked into the woods, and opened my hands
I dug a whole not far in the ground and buried my notebook
And pen without sound; what I wrote came from earth
I returned my blessings to comfort her
I took the back roads home Saturday night

Serpent Seven
Wanna share a secret?
Painted with your smile
Me, and you and my emotional dial
Just spin my wheel
And I'll laugh, cry or kneel
Your heaven on earth
And I wanna cop-a-feel!

Demetria HotChocolate Fails
There's a light at the end of the tunnel
But I'm gonna have to fight my way out of it
And I hope you'll be waiting at the end for me
I was fighting to get to you in the end. ♥

Demetria HotChocolate Fails

Let me be the one to be your wife;
Let me be the one that you share everything with;
I wanna be the centre of your world
And be the only girl ♥

Demetria HotChocolate Fails

I long for the day to kiss your lips
To feel your breath
To feel you arms wrap around me like a straightjacket;
To listen to your heart beat
Like a beautiful beat to a great song in my ear

Demetria HotChocolate Fails

He makes my heart skip a beat or two;
Quite funny but true
Just listening to him laugh makes me smile for a little while;
What makes him special?
His carefree spirit, his laid back charm
A joke that he doesn't have to work too hard to make me laugh at ♥

Jude Joneson

Sitting here I have cried my eyes out
Day after day for the past eight months
Depression and anxiety have taken a toll on my weak focus of life.
I wonder how my medication is helping me
I ponder how I got to this point in my life
At this point the eight months have become only a day...a major blur
I cry and stay at home, afraid to be happy... afraid to love
Feeling my life beginning to crumble more and more...
Afraid that my life will suddenly end and no one will care

Njabulo Preacher S Makhanya

Maybe it's not the relationship at all that's driving you dilly
Maybe you've had enough
The trick is not to abandon ship
It's not sinking, it needs to steer a new course
You are the reason the sun got up today
Believe it for the last time in the year

Serpent Seven

Oh where, oh where did my angel go?
Maybe across town, maybe to, and fro
Maybe she's somewhere picking dandelions for her hair
Maybe she's in an alley making out with bear?
I really don't know, but my halo broke,
And I'm provoked to host my throat
Oh where, oh where, did my angel go?

Serpent Seven

You bested me
I am no longer just one

When the dust settles I'd even bare you a son
For 21 years I've lived alone
And now my love involves you Hun
I used to only do for me
My selfish ways, my insecurities
But now it's true, I'm blue without my boo
It's you, for truth, my mystery sloth

Njabulo Preacher S Makhanya

Sometimes pure frustration is a lesson in itself
You've done what needed to be done
And the goodies failed to pitch
There's a right time and there's your time
Don't let those who aren't in tune with you distract you from those who are

Molly Maharaj

From my heart to yours

A year is almost over
A journey lost in time
Dreams lost and found
A time to take a moment to recall promises made
A time to pick the broken pieces
And mend roads long forgotten
Nobody knows what tomorrow holds
Nobody knows if they'll wake to see the new dawn
But today is here, with memories shared
And hopes to make anew the scars of yesteryear
These lines I write for the ones like me
Who wonder still in the hope to find the answers yet not found
The seasons not yet enjoyed, the dreams still not made real
People my people far and wide...on this journey in time
I love u all...God bless u on your journey

Njabulo Preacher S Makhanya

The planets are playing, rocking a few boats. Minimise the definite plans, and maximise the work on yourself. Believe it or not, this level of drama can be loads of fun. Impatience and a fear of failure are the things that trip you up.

Njabulo Preacher S Makhanya

Let go of something you're used to. It will bring sadness, relief and confusion. It's time for change. It doesn't really matter what, as long as you change. If you're focused on revenge you'd better take up boxing.

Serpent Seven
You never cease to amaze, how you craze me
Through mind, body; my soul has no choice but to follow
Like a slave to its master I'm captured
Your tongue is the most powerful persuader
You bring me mountains of gushy-lust with each thrust and true favours
No girl's dignity is braver
During the day I savoured
What became of me last night and my behaviour?
What becomes of me tonight?
Not even god's favours in site
What you do to me
So I'm here on all fours, begging to be your sore whore
Well you bate me? Will you take me? Only the wind knows as it blows...
And I wait for my fate on your floor

Serpent Seven

Make my stay for it
Make me pray for it
Bound tight in this swing
Masked, and waiting on you to bring me pleasure
Whenever you decide to cum
What fun when twirled and spun?

Bernart Jules Harris

Birdz of Prey (B.O.P)

The Birdz of Prey formed, once the Killer Beez swarmed
Came to post up on the tree of life
The beez in their hives
The birdz perched in their nests
Hip-Hop they manifest
The group consists of 8 members

The ultimate goal of the group is to bring the truth to the music

Serpent Seven
You cling to my breast, like a well nourished newborn
Licking and sucking my life's essence for your very, selfish, own
You always have, and always will
I know that now, and time never stands still
But it doesn't really matter to me
I'd give you my air, for you to breathe
As I wilt away, you grow stronger
Filling yourself with my dignity and honour
I happily and with open arm release my life into your palms
My reasons for living have never meant so little
as I close my eyes upon your pillow
You smile as I try to gather what's left
I cling to you as I slowly accept death
Serpent Seven
Most of my muse is bits and pieces of previous writings of done
Experiences, feelings, and personal emotions seem to be my basis
Somehow, they just all seem to come out/back when I write
It pulls out of me right onto the paper so I don't go and do something foolish
Or stupid, a release, or outlet if you will;
Necessary, mental, climatic, moments in my short life
Often I find myself holding back
Or not totally forthcoming when I write on FB
I have been threatened, followed, stalked, ridiculed, labelled a devil worshiper
And once an attempted exorcism by a so-called on-line priest!
For me, writing is really about a journey back to what's real
Or what is considered reality here, here in society
I often, cognitively, and slowly/daily get into these states of blankness
Or unreal/unrest, and it wreaks havoc on my personal and professional life
Writing lets me bridge the gap safely between my realities and my mind
If I didn't write, they would blur, or mix violently
And eventually consume me with them
LOL, an exorcism wouldn't be too far off the mark then
So for me writing is necessary for survival
I have known this for a long time and embrace it
However I haven't championed it yet
That is my personal goal for me
So, until then, here I am, bleeding and writing, for all to see and read

Serpent Seven
You move my hair, as you stare and I R.E.M. away on an island, far
Just me, you and the stars, holding hands by day, fishing by night
No clock to chain to No boss to fight

My heart floats in-between your arms
Laughing from one-liners and all of your charms
And then I wake to find you not there
By my lonesome, not strong enough to bare
I weep god's prayer seven fold. You never reveal yourself, truth be told

Serpent Seven
You`re here for me again, an eventful, rapist, trend
I'm young and innocent;
You greet me as a friend
Quick to see, I'm just another mare for you to share
You split me to my core, I scream as a breathe;
You treat me as a whore
I grin and I bare it
Afterwards, you kiss my head and tear it
I'm shaking and bleeding from cardinal sin
You don't spare it
You spit on me, and laugh
Brash as you butcher it
I cry out in a deafening, silent sound
And I thought you'd marry it!

Njabulo Preacher S Makhanya

Let go of something you're used to
It will bring sadness, relief and confusion
It's time for change now
It doesn't really matter what, as long as you change
If you're focused on revenge, you would better take up boxing

Serpent Seven

Magnificent man in a pan
With a spray on tan
No FAM, no ham
Just himself and his hands
How selfish you are
By your own drinks at the bar
I don't need a man with a tan
I have my own lovely, soft, moisten, hands!

Serpent Seven

Today, I remember
To be thankful for what?
On that dreaded day, you washed my family away
My Father pushed me to higher ground as he drowned
My Mother was swept away, her body later found
Why god did you spare me?
Why god, to watch me bleed?
So here I lay, no arms to pray
No legs to walk I'll just slither away
Out of your body, out of your light
No thanks again, from you tonight

Jude Joneson

Through the darkness, I can see your light and you will always shine
I can feel your heart in mine
Your face I've memorized and I idolize just you
There is peace in my soul
For such a long awaited time
There is love in my life
A love of melody and rhyme
Once you took hold of my heart
I knew no other could have reached
As whispered fate took my hand
To levels only you could reach.
You in my life
Will live eternally
I knew the first night we met
You were meant for me
I don't know how to say this.
the words walking through my mind.
I can't put pen to paper,
the sentence I can't find,
for the feelings deep inside my heart.
I pray to God above.
for the right words to tell you,
how much I have fallen in love
As I sit here and daydream
Of the first day we met
I can still see your eyes gleam
And I feel as if I won a bet
You're mine to keep
For now and forever
I love you with all my heart
Our love is so deep

It's as if we are a piece of art
So I'm yours and you are mine

Jude Joneson

Yesterday love was simple
Two lives sharing memories
Today it is more complicated
Starting over is scary and unsettling
Loving another makes me anxious and cautious
Love has always been love, yet can I return it?
Can I now accept it with no limitations?
Strangely, I feel taken advantage of.
Love has no boundaries or guarantees.
I am no longer interested in forever.
Passion sparks at inopportune moments
Waiting around makes me impatient and unyielding
Why has love become an unspoken word that is felt and not returned?
Was yesterday forever and can today be yesterday?

Mlungisi Makhanya

Love one Another - The knowledge that God has loved me beyond all limits will compel me to go into
the world to love others in the same way. Love is spontaneous, but it has to be maintained through
discipline. ♥ Yoll all!!!!!!!!!!!!!

Molly Maharaj

Listen my friend, Listen to the cries
Of your brethren across the miles
Hark, they all sound the same.
The cry of hunger, the cry of pain
Of unheard voices
Crying out in vain
When will we learn, When will we see
The painful pleas
Have no colour or creed

Serpent Seven

I am your marionette.
Move my strings, and I'll dance for you.
Whenever you want, I'm here for you.
My permanent smile, my emotional pile,
Play second best to your cognitive mile.
I am your marionette!

Molly Maharaj

You have the Power
The magic within
To change your surroundings
Bring smiles to all u meet
Take up the challenge
Make a stand today
To smile at a stranger
Even if not returned
Bless the one who horns at you
Tell yourself he knows you not
His anger is somewhere else
Pray he finds his peace within
We're on a journey
You and I, Travelling the untrodden
Journey called life
Have a Wonderful Day My Friends

Kynthia I. Thisbe

"It is only with the heart that one can see a pure love; what is essential to the mind in these matters is invisible to the eye. And words never spoken are as tainted as actions never followed through so turned to lies. It's easier to respect when one is straight forward with which way they choose to turn if dealing with you too; otherwise I wouldn't give a damn, if you want to follow a path to who knows where the hell to" KIT

Kynthia I. Thisbe

"Should we confess all our mistakes to one another, if not just for the laughter it would cause for our lack of originality? Or would we for once see we are at times on the same road together even through our journey individually? I always question ways to bridge the gap so that we may be as a true "one love" someday in history long enough to be written in stone even if I am passed. For the children I will leave behind, my nieces and nephews deserve to know I at least tried." KIT

Molly Maharaj

A diplomat is someone who can tell you to go to hell in such a way that you will look forward to the trip.

Donna Osborn Clark

"Extraordinary is the "extra" that makes us more than ordinary. The "extra" that you have is your gift that will make you shine in HIS brilliant light once you share it with the world." ~ Donna Osborn Clark

Kynthia I. Thisbe

"To love with a shattered heart and fell many times to my knees if not further; yet still I will always reach for the stars, whatever happens -happens but not without a fight from within the depths of me." KIT

Sherry Weaver
"Darkness inside my head"
When I see them all around
I can't believe what I found,
I found the way to visit-
Even when they're dead
I found them in a little room-
Locked inside my head

When I opened up that door
I saw the ones, who lived no more,
I saw their fate, their deep abyss-
I saw the ones, - I truly missed
I came across a place for me,
Where death is truly life,
I found it, the place to see
All the death and broken dreams,
All the darkness and tragedies,
All that passed before my eyes.
Even here in my head
It's full of pain, mixed with dread,
My lifeless soul, now dark and dead

Solomon Kalushi Mahlangu

During Heritage month its whereby we should be celebrating the discipline and history of our people and evolution of society as it is driven by the NDR and we build this NDS we should embrace character and principles of the forefather likes of OR Tambo, W.Sisulu, S.Mahlangu, Moses Mabhida, Chris Hani, Bantu Bike, Sabelo Phama, Nelson Mandela, Ruth First, Lillian Ngoyi, Winnie Mandela....Amandla...celebrate the history of Dubula ibhunu, rise and come back again the forefathers spirits..Of leadership...Long Live ANC,long live...

Molly Maharaj

A Cry in the Wild written 1997

The voice of Justice cries out in me
Break out of this Corruption fate we see
Make a statement show your stand
Sit not wondering what the plan is

General discussions and silent pleas
Can't make a future for you or me
We have a right in this world to be
We're not alone you will see

The road is long that's for sure
With many a turn and many a stone
But success has never in time been won
On wistful thinking and idle dreaming

Jessica DayRodriguez
Black Crow Blue -

The fever broke, but the other side of sickness would
Never know wellness truly
I didn't mean to but I became the kind of person that knows
Themselves so well that everyone else would remain a stranger
So to move like a worm under the earth without any need for eyes
Nothing to see just feel; feel all my hurt pleasuring at times
Gradually I watch it happen, seeds that become
Blades of grass poking out from the sand
Like the dirty needles plunged in my heart also creating the poison,
That slips through my veins
All my loves are suicide and all my lovers a simple razor blade.
Drink me now like a sweet aged glass of wine that love also ferments
The same way and grows more intoxicating day by day.

Jaimal Anand

The mist in the forest is a strange phenomena, only if you been in a snowy, sub zero alpine forest
would you know that feeling, as armies once set up camp, soldiers enduring the anxiety of the
looming battle at dawn, the darkness only broken by the rays of the full moon shimmering through
the thick of the wood. The smell in the air is a strange combination of the aroma of glory, and the
stench of fear, armies throughout history have felt this....jackals in the distance, the hoot of an owl,
the whisper of the breeze through the trees- like life, waiting for the dawn, we feel fear, but the mild
rays of moonlight sooth the grimness, make the jackals sound les like an evil omen and the hoot of
an owl becomes comforting....did I dream this last night...I did...but I also remember my late night
wintery walks and drives in those alpine mountains.....

Jessica DayRodriguez

"Being alone isn't the worst thing; I have been in isolation now 7 years... Still you get lied to, hurt, shattered, though no one sees the tears. The worst thing is knowing you stay alive for everyone else, but not once were they in my shoes to see how much it hurts. But I'm the selfish one just begging every night that I will not wake with the morning light and get my wish come true." JDR

Jessica DayRodriguez

Your parasitic body -

Often when we don't get the rest we need,
We question things we already achieved or conquered long before.
The miserable "what-ifs" that we were satisfied, come creeping back into the door.
With every neglectful thing you push your body through; it fights back by trying
To convince you to regret what you never did before.
I have said your body is a parasite always killing the spirit of your soul
Feed it what it wants, even if you have to force it down as an anorexic would do
Otherwise the host suffers an unfixable damage leaving nothing but
A scared body of battle wounds
Awaiting the exit door to where
The lost regain their strength and willpower once more.
In order to move back to what they didn't learn before

Jude Joneson
Gentle breezes whisper as I linger
The area where the accident happened is just a blur in my mind
Somehow I am expecting closure but am overwhelmed at the way things could of been..
The scene has an aura of tranquillity and patience
think my patience is there with his spirit trying to comfort him somehow...
Loving him was a challenge
An unyielding demand still tries to torment my soul..
Memories flood my mind and streams of tears are flowing down my cheeks.
My senses are exploding with anguish and despair...
Because living with him was a bigger challenge.
My heart holds much compassion for him still and yet oddly just need this closure to say good bye
friend, sorry you had to leave so soon,
Hope you get to where you think you should be but think you will...
I hold no grudges anymore; this is my closure I get to carry on...
Yet I oddly remember mixed emotions I kiss the bouquet sit it down by the pole and turn away......
Good night my friend, good night my love....

Akhona Qabaka
Lost identity

I lost my identity the day i was flooded with rhymes and verses in my mind. Asking Who am I? I said I lost my identity when I first laid my stick in the wisdom buried between her thighs. She asked who am I. I am he who tells the tales that unties the chain to unlocks the pain buried in the inside. Who am I? I am he who was lost in thoughts while they were seeking and searching for my wisdom they couldn't find no evil as I had more visions than they could imagine in one season. They searched and searched but the vessel was empty didn't have nothing no clue but missiles. Now that we even you might as well call me doctor Evil. Who am i? I am the devil worst enemy born to destroy the discouragement planted in the less courage minds so you can call me the Devil himself. Yes I said it, call me the devil himself but I'm not the Devil I'm just a person who lost his identity. Again I ask Who am i? I was found on earth, lived on earth, bled the sense of being perfected by the streets on earth. Whu am i?I was not born out of the woman's womb though my body was inside her womb for 9 months.I was made by the pain that reside with the stain in darkest allis, sold my soul to be pefected in the dark so call me the dark side of you. Whu em i?I am founded where no one wants to gobut imagination always find a way to bore big holes through the thicker boundaries between our worlds. Whu em i? I am the lost soul.I am the lost soul. The lost i am, i lost my identity.Yes i said i lost my identity. I lost my identity when they first cut my umbilcal cord from the wonderful source that is my mother. I lost my identity when they slaughter the lamb in celebrating my arrival and my being as a human being. I lost my identity when i first saw that tear drop in my mama's eyes when they read my death sentence. Nyan they sentenced me to deathThey sentenced me to death for my domestic unhuman deeds. This is only whats left of my human identity.Lost identity

Jude Joneson

Choices

I find myself sitting in my room with tears streaming down my face.

Tears are flowing without emotion as I remember

You are I were meant to be one, but rage has stopped our connection.

You are beyond reasoning with...

Beating another is a control thing..sadly I ask,

but why?

What have I ever done to you, besides love you?

Can I ever please you?

Can our children and love change your desire and attitude?

I used to think I could but now I know...

Life is not as simplistic as i hoped it would be

get married and raise a family...not happening I see.

You have a rage in your soul that is beyond control..Beat me again if you must but remember one thing life has a way of kicking your ass back when you behave like this...

I sit and wait patiently...hoping someday I will be free.

Love has turned into hate and torment

Love is mine to give and I no longer choose yours...

So here I sit crying behind closed doors

Lindsay Athiemulam

Cradle me oh Africa, please do - Somalian Baby

Laying on her lap, a pillow made of bones

Ears so far but I hear her hearts groans

I can hear the words "I'm sorry" so loud

She says she failed me

She says she tried

She says when I was born, she never thought of the day I would die

All this spoken without a word

How she wishes i was never detached from my umbilical cord

Wanted me to have a blankie as blue as the blue skies

Now, my blankie, the one I have, is made of flies

Cradle me oh Africa as I lay dying

Cradle my mommy as I hear her heart crying

Jude Joneson

My mother played piano

And I would dance.

When our house caught fire,

I mimicked the flames with the arch of my body.

My mother stared solidly into the blaze.

Molly Maharaj

The care of human life and happiness, and not their destruction, is the 1st and only legitimate object of good governance

Jaimal Anand 'Through the darkness, I can see your light and you will always shine' now that is indeed a quotable quote....as for the rest...GENIUS

Love one Another - The knowledge that God has loved me beyond all limits will compel me to go into the world to love others in the same way. Love is spontaneous, but it has to be maintained through discipline. ♥ you all!! Mlungisi Makhanya

Serpent Seven

I am your marionette.

Move my strings, and I'll dance for you.

Whenever you want, I'm here for you.

My permanent smile, my emotional pile,

Play second best to your cognitive mile.

I am your marionette!

Thecla Shozi

B The Man

Be d man and sing along to d unwanted pleasures of 2 hands beating a drum!!!

Working simultaneously in melody, not making a song of love but one of lust...

So b d man and say your song, was a song of pain!!!

Dedicated to me!!!

"Your children are not your children. They are the sons and daughters of life's longing for itself. They come through you, but not from you. Though they are with you, yet they belong not to you. You may give them your love but not your thoughts. You may house their bodies, but not their souls. You may strive to be like them but seek not to make them like you." Molly Maharaj

"U have the Power, The magic within, to change your surroundings, Bring smiles to all u meet. Take up the challenge; Make a stand today, to smile at a stranger, Even if not returned. Bless the one who horns at u, Tell yourself he knows u not, His anger is somewhere else, Pray he finds his peace within. We're on a journey, U and I, Travelling the untraded, Journey called life" Molly Maharaj

It's a good time to fulfil ambitions & get what you ordered but try not to get ahead of yourself. Everything at the office is on track, almost as if it was specially designed to meet your needs. The more you give, the more you'll receive. Njabulo Preacher S Makhanya

That point between dark and light, that twilight...that place...I like it...you may ask why..but for some of us we hurt others...are forgiven....and go on living....victims live with that hurt for life.....who is selfish and who is honest....I think I'm selfish Jaimal Anand

"Creative surges are being dampened by a demand for structure & discipline. Don't fight it off. There are many ways to focus without losing the flow. Everyone has something to teach you." Njabulo Preacher S Makhanya

"It is only with the heart that one can see a pure love; what is essential to the mind in these matters is invisible to the eye. And words never spoken are as tainted as actions never followed through so turned to lies. It's easier to respect when one is straight forward with which way they choose to turn if dealing with you too; otherwise I wouldn't give a damn, if you want to follow a path to who knows where the hell to" KIT

"Should we confess all our mistakes to one another, if not just for the laughter it would cause for our lack of originality? Or would we for once see we are at times on the same road together even through our journey individually? I always question ways to bridge the gap so that we may be as a true "one love" someday in history long enough to be written in stone even if I am passed. For the children I will leave behind, my nieces and nephews deserve to know I at least tried." KIT

A diplomat is someone who can tell you to go to hell in such a way that you will look forward to the trip. Molly Maharaj

"Extraordinary is the "extra" that makes us more than ordinary. The "extra" that you have is your gift that will make you shine in HIS brilliant light once you share it with the world." ~ Donna Osborn Clark

"To love with a shattered heart and fell many times to my knees if not further; yet still I will always reach for the stars, whatever happens -happens but not without a fight from within the depths of me." KIT

Jaimal Anand

The mist in the forest is a strange phenomenon
Only if you been in a snowy, sub zero alpine forest
Would you know that feeling
As armies once set up camp, soldiers enduring the anxiety of the looming battle at dawn
The darkness only broken by the rays of the full moon shimmering through the thick of the wood
The smell in the air is a strange combination of the aroma of glory, and the stench of fear
Armies throughout history have felt this
Jackals in the distance, the hoot of an owl, the whisper of the breeze through the trees- like life
Waiting for the dawn, we feel fear, but the mild rays of moonlight sooth the grimness
Make the jackals sound less like an evil omen and the hoot of an owl becomes comforting
Did I dream this last night...I did...but I also remember my late night wintery walks and drives
In those alpine mountains

Jaimal Anand

Just 3 questions

Is pain a sensation, a feeling or just a figment of our imagination, like fear or anxiety....?
Can we feel empathy or sympathy without knowing pain.....?
Are we just fools and slaves to our thoughts...?

Author Otis Randolf
Good morning heartache
I see you brewed two cups of coffee
I was surprised to see that you rendezvoused with me in my dreams last night
A foolish dream or a fool's dream? Which one was it?
A little of both? You're probably right.
Sbongile MaMkhize Dolwana
DADDY IN HEAVEN

"It's been a year Daddy; I really, really miss you.
Mommy says, 'you safe now in a beautiful place called Heaven'
We are having your favourite dinner tonight
I ate it all up, even though I don't like carrots
I learned how to swim this summer
I can even hold open my eyes when I m under water
Can't you see me? I've started at kindergarten this year
I`m carrying a picture of us like booze, crooze and pass
You are the greatest daddy I can swing all by myself now even though I miss you pushing me
Can't you see me?
I miss how you used to tickle me, tickle my belly, my belly hurts
I try not to cry-mommy says, it's ok
I know you don't like it when I cry
You never wanted me to be scared
I try daddy but its hurts
It is true you're not coming home, maybe someday I could visit you in Heaven ok?
It's time for me to go to bed now, I sleep with lights on
Just in case you come home and kiss me goodnight
I miss you so much, I love you daddy

Jessica DayRodriguez

Star Lover -

How carefully I watched the strength and independence you seemed to carry in both hands

As you carried me into the woman who has left you smiling and misty

While I travelled so many miles away to study the physics of the universe

Thank god the stars aligned to bring you to me, though farther from you I am now

Closer and closer to you the stars bring me

Jessica DayRodriguez

"Being alone isn't the worst thing; I have been in isolation now 7 years...

Still you get lied to, hurt, shattered, though no one sees the tears

The worst thing is knowing you stay alive for everyone else

But not once were they in my shoes to see how much it hurts

But I'm the selfish one just begging every night that I will not wake with the morning light

and get my wish come true." JDR

My spoken word piece has been added Author Otis Randolf

Jude Joneson

Gentle breezes whisper as I linger
The area where the accident happened is just a blur in my mind
Somehow I am expecting closure but am overwhelmed at the way things could of been
The scene has an aura of tranquillity and patience
Think my patience is there with his spirit trying to comfort him somehow

AmaTainted Titles
That stanza has yet to form
Sometimes one has to leave things open ended
Because of confusion or to being not quite ready to step away from the scene
All in due time... when this bird finds her wings, she will soar

A life time of experience take a life time to spit, when all is said and done you not done, your life is a chain of miracles Mlungisi Makhanya

Lindsay Athiemulam

Cradle me oh Africa, please do - Somalian Baby
Lying on her lap, a pillow made of bones
Ears so far but I hear her hearts groans
I can hear the words "I'm sorry" so loud

Lindsay Athiemulam

My footprint, fingerprint, DNA it is my identification
My existence, breathe, heart beat it is my life
My hurt, pain, love, laughter it is my emotions

All of these belong to me. Mine.
My innocence, my trust, my hope, my happiness, my future it is Mine
Sbongile MaMkhize Dolwana
Smooth roads never make good drivers
Calm seas never make good sailors
Clear skies never make good pilots
A problem free life never makes a good person
Be strong enough to accept the challenges of life
Just say "With God by my side TRY ME"

Jude Joneson
Since the day we met, I've grown so deeply in love with you
Day by day, my love for you becomes so overwhelming
Till I can't handle it when I don't see or talk to you for even one day
You make me feel wonderful
You give me strength when I just can't carry on
You make me laugh and laugh a lot and I truly treasure that
I can never imagine how it would be like if we were to lose each other
O don't even want to think of it, Baby
All I want to think of is you
You are the love of my life
May God bless your beautiful soul
From the bottom of my heart, I love you

"To love is life, to be loved is something beautiful, but to be loved by the one you love is...everything
pure! ♥" JDR
Jude Joneson

I sit here in sorrow, wishing I could hold you
I've realized that I've tried to replace you
Ever since I made the foolish decision to leave you
But, no one can make me laugh and smile like you do
You are the only one that ever made me so happy
No one could ever take your place
I feel as if my soul has stolen my heart and left me to cry myself to sleep
Each and every night with guilt in my heart of how I have hurt you
I guess you just don't realize what you have till after it's gone
I was so stupid to leave you
I know sorry is just a word, but for what it's worth I am very sorry
And I beg you with every breath of my soul
"Please forgive me and I want you to know I think about you every day and night"
When I am with you, you light up my life
You are the best thing that has ever happened to me
And I wish upon a star for you to return back to my side
The love that I hold for you in my soul is greater than the ocean or the sky above

Please forgive me for all the hurt that I have caused you
Please, I beg of you to forgive me and return back to my side
Like the way it was meant to be
I love you and will always love you till the day that I die
Jude Joneson
Baby, from the moment I met you
I knew you were someone special to me
I knew by the way you looked at me, talked to me was there for me
I was afraid to love again...afraid of the pain it might bring
But in a short time, you showed me that real love wasn't painful or deceiving
You showed me that I deserved to be loved and happy
You gave new meaning to my life and I could never thank you enough for that
You are truly a Godsend to me!
Jude Joneson
How did I ever get so lucky?
Loneliness was a pain I felt in my heart
The same pain we both felt
Thank God he led us to be together
Because we are now a family
Love is the only house that is big enough for all the pain in the world
There you are in the stillness of the night
When I'm looking for the light
Looking for the brightest star and there you are
You stand alone above anyone; you light up my world and complete my being
Simply, you are the love of my life and I just wanted to remind you that I love you!
Lindsay Athiemulam
Day Dreamer takes me away from here
Places my body right next to yours
Mouth saying what it should
All things that were locked up comes out and feels good
It takes me to a bench where I sit and have a conversation with you
Sharing this dream that I once had that has come true
Sun on our faces, warming up our hearts
In this place we will never be apart
A paradise created just for us
Nothing that shakes this earth would shake us
Nothing that has been barriers for so long longer exists
A paradise created a moment in time that just stands still
Day dreamer that never wants to awake
A day dreamer, my own paradise I create

Lindsay Athiemulam

Woman in the corner Woman in the corner
Face busted, body bruised

Pain not only running through your body
Your child's heart too
Consider the worst that would happen if you walk away
Consider the impact on your baby's future if you change your life today
Stand up, scream, and shout, "NO LONGER AS A PUNCHING BAG I'LL BE USED"
Teach your child that pain is not part of love
That abuse is not part of love
Consider the possibility that maybe you could be happy without fear
Consider that your son will grow up to hold a woman dearly
You were born complete woman in the corner
You were born whole
You were born to be loved
You were born to be taken care of
You were born to be a caregiver to your child
Consider your face busted and body bruised
Consider that all the considering might be done from your casket
Consider your child without a caregiver
Consider yourself DEAD!!!Woman in the corner, face busted, body bruised
Stand up, scream, and shout "NO LONGER YOUR PUNCHING BAG, TIME TO TAP OUT."
Serpent Seven
I won't rush, blush, or cuss
I'll be right here
Waiting for him hibernating like a bear
Waiting for his signs, his cold winter blows
When there's no more rain, just wonderful, white snow
My favourite season of all, my frozen emotional wall
So here I'll lay bare, in my comfortable lair
Dreaming.... of tomorrow, don't wake me

Lindsay Athiemulam

The unknown

Not really searching for something familiar
Tired of the old but not easy to accept the change
The new and nor the unknown
I open the door to my home
The smell of your fragrance fills the air
Pause and shake my head
Someone in my space
Moving closer to the room where the scent gets stronger
Turn and run, my head tells my heart
I can't, I'm just floating on air not away from you
But towards you and there is absolutely nothing that I can do
Fight it, my head says, the unknown,
The shadow that is moving closer down that passage might not be good for you

Yet I need it, want to be totally surrounded by it
Want to be swallowed in by the shadow
The unknown it might be, yes
Not sure of what tomorrow holds for us
Not knowing how it would end
What I do know though is the feeling I feel now
This feeling was UNKNOWN too
If the unknown of tomorrow feels as good as the LOVE I know today
Then so be it Not easy to accept not easy to understand but no fear for the unknown

Serpent Seven
Here I lay
Surrounded by derivational dandelions in my hidden garden
Away from cars and smog, people and malls waiting
Stripped of cloth and conviction
Waiting for a sign

Waiting for you to enter me one more time
Like an uncontrolled orgasm you arrive
Forced, and full of hope, words and song
I tremble in delight until all that's dark is light
Reborn, with open mind, body and spirit,
Accepting your every whim,

Filled with foetus, and tears of joy
Mixing with fluid from my soul and flesh
It is conceived!
Alive and well, derived from heaven and hell
Healthy and hungry, I nourish and cherish her until she's ready for the world to listen
Can you hear me?

Serpent Seven

Marry Poppins! No one's stopping` her
She is what she does.
Without binge, or buzz
So, why am I the alpha grudge?
I'm no different; it's all in her name.
And if I change mine, will I feel the same?
In Marry Poppins, stockings

Serpent Seven

If I jump, will it make a difference?
It hurts more sometimes, when you're so specific.
I know, it's my fault again. I'm a bad little girl; this skin I'm in
Will you miss me?

My puppet smile?

My emotional pile?
My mono-toned style?
I don't think so, not even for a second, and so for you I have a present
I jump 30 stories tall, aiming for your car to break my fall

"Swans gathered in three in the shallow water, as

elephants washed at the water's edge seemly below" I really like that bit....but moreso 'one line was all he drew' is a line that probably has more meaning in every dot that makes the line.....than a canvass filled...Jaimal Anand

In the eye of the political storm, calm rests, but in the rage that follows chaos looms,

When the tide of glory rises, it forgets that it must recede at that command of the moon,

When the bliss of peace is upon us, we believe that pax is eternal

I have this view , that world in which we live can only be governed by to dialectic forces, the law of nature, and the reason of man,

Both forces, have never, and will never be in balance, as fear, courage, ambition, dogma, humility and pride drive our every effort as individuals Jaimal Anand

PONDER THIS

"Sometimes the only person you can trust is yourself"

"Life is not about waiting for the storm to pass, it is about dancing in the rain"

"Behind every bitch is a guy who made them be"

"Think I`m tripping tie my shoes"Mlungisi Makhanya

Yeah, who said blood is thicker than water, when it is full of liquor it becomes thin while the water is still full of natural chemicals.Mlungisi Makhanya

Sitting in that chair and saying what's on your mind. I know all about that. Don Gayelit

Resentment

By Tragedy L. Dark, TLD

I gave you an out, you choose to stay in. Now I wondering if you made the right choice to begin . A person unable to see pass the past will never see the bright future ahead. I admit I've made wrong choices and occasionally been the fool but under no circumstances was that your cue to be rude. Strong to the world but for you I was broken, battered, and weak I was definitely yours but you made no attempt to keep. When I had enough realizing my heart had failed me for the last time I was willing to allow it, I walked away defeated had down, white flag drawn and you convinced me to stay. Truth is you weren't sure how to love me or if you could love me, you just didn't want anybody else to love me. My complaints, my pleas and cries fell on selectively hearing deaf ears; other saw heard them and wanted to be there. My resentment build higher and higher because you were the only one I wanted to care. Resentment because you had an out stayed in but it never felt like you were near.

EVERY SUNRISE AND EVERY SUNSET

With every sunrise and sunset, there are a series of events that unfold that we call our day, the events that unfold have, in my view, two characteristics, one we can never reverse those events, and two the events are surprises that either embrace us with warmth and care or bombard us like rockets.

With every sunrise and sunset, we have a choices, we can choose to allow these events destabilise us, or we can choose to welcome each event, good and bad, what is our daily choice...do we really know what to do with the unknown....living is just a constant surprise, and we react to those surprises with actions that we cannot change ....or can we?

Every sunrise and every sunset.....brings actions, every action creates events, all these events put together we call our lives...or is it?"Jaimal Anand

NEVER LET THE DOG GUARDS A BONE" Mlungisi Makhanya

Fear, pain, and regret

Are forever with me

They torment me while I sleep

And consume when I awake.

I hide behind masks hoping Rochelle Kotzé

You are really in a prison which is called the fear...

Free your mind. Don Gayelit

There is always a struggle between the brain and one`s heart when it comes to matters of the heart. But eventually you will listen to your heart. Don Gayelit

"WINNERS NEVER QUIT, QUITORS NEVER WIN" Mlungisi Makhanya

Is not every day that we are at our best abilities, not every night that the Moon in us shines nor daily we get sun rays and wind clouds too neither need the rays no guarantee that daily in August it will be dusty... Is not everyone who will Love, appreciate and accept us in the same way nor that every person will not want to see where we stepped.... Nor Monthly that our Bank accounts will rain superior they too flood of inferiority as much we enjoy Sunny days we have to keep it in mind that cold snowy days are bound to came as we plant new trees on the other side of town another tree is being cut down to make fire for warmness nor every new Born is born Crying and is not in our Heart to see fellow Human being hurting above all this GOD LOVES US ALL NO MATTER WHAT!

"FRANKNESS AND SINCERITY ALWAYS FRIGHTEN PEOPLE A LITTLE, THEY GET A FEELING THAT YOU MIGHT GO TOO FAR"Mlungisi Makhanya

WITH A DIAMOND AT HAND SHE JUST DISSOLVED ON HER SEAT SHE SUCCUMBED TO HIS ILLUSSION AND GAVE UP EVERYTHING...MLUNGISI MAKHANYA

Tragedy L. Dark (TLD) The Bedroom Bully was born and raised in Harlem. He is an upcoming author of erotic and urban short stor